A New Way to Learn English

Peter D. Ward

Table of Contents:

End of Part I

Discussion Scenarios (153 in all)
(They can be done in any order; some may not be
suitable for every student or class.)

In Other Words: This section contains articles
to help the vocabulary of students. Each article is
written twice. The second one has more difficult
vocabulary. The selections are of different
length. Some will take up more than one page.

A New Way to Learn English: Preface

"The world is not waiting for another English textbook. "Those are the 'encouraging' words I heard from friends when they found out I was writing a textbook. As you see from the finished product, I did not agree with them. After teaching for over 50 years, I can honestly say I have never found a perfect textbook. Of course this text is not perfect either, but I believe it is useful and needed.

A textbook should be like a crutch. It helps for a short time, but it should not be used forever. So this text is to help people grasp or review the basics and then continue to make progress by themselves. Its aim is to provide a framework for developing and continuing a conversation. Consequently, learning how to think is better than spending a life time memorizing someone else's thoughts. This text relies on thinking and imagination to make it valuable. By realizing how sentences are related, students will find it easy to make their own connections.

Conversation means sharing one's ideas, experiences, questions, and comments. This does not mean that one has to be a slave to a text. If a student's conversation is the same as that in a textbook, it means that he/she has the same DNA as the writer, and or is the writer's twin brother or sister! There are few sentences or words that must be said in a given scenario. Speakers are free to make their own association of ideas. So learning to use one's imagination is far more important than learning the contents of a textbook - even this one. What are provided here are just many examples, primarily using imagination together with some useful sentence patterns.

Use of frameworks. When one speaks one's native language, one relies on a framework to continue talking.

 The speaker will add to the conversation by adding reasons, results, feelings, experiences, comparisons, and other aspects of the topic. This is done quickly and subconsciously in one's own language, so that the speaker is often not even conscious he/she is using them. One can easily use the 'Wh- framework to lengthen a conversation. This means adding sentences to explain why, when, where, what, who, how, how many or how much. One can usually add a 'wh-' sentence to most single sentences in English.

Students of English must learn to say what they can say, not what they want to say. This means using words one knows to get ideas across to others. It does not consist in translating one's first language into English or vice versa. If this technique is not learned, one can study English forever. Learn from kindergarten children; they talk incessantly even though their vocabulary is very limited. The secret is to learn English to use, not to study English just to know it!

Another important hint is first explaining yourself in easy words rather than trying to memorize vocabulary lists. Learn to explain difficult words using easy words. After all, every day English conversation usually uses no more than 3,000 words.

This text provides a blueprint for studying by changing the way to learn English. Any English teacher, no matter how incompetent, can open a text and explain it. That does not mean that the student is learning anything, or that he or she will ever feel confident speaking English. The real test of English ability is if a student can converse about a topic with an English speaker. The aim of this text is to make students conscious of thought patterns which they use unconsciously in their own language. Learning how to learn is equally as important as learning English. It is important not to confuse the two.

The text will have a few test pages to teach basic patterns/sentences so that students can test themselves. Grammar is included but in useful pattern contexts. When a speaker makes many small grammar mistakes, it usually distracts the listener. So we have provided a few practical exercises to reinforce grammar rules. Some difficult vocabulary is explained but it is only introduced in useful contexts. Words should never be learned in lists; usually they will be forgotten in less than 24 hours.

This book will demonstrate how learning takes place and it will facilitate the student's grasp of concepts, and act as a true catalyst for learning and thinking. The end of the book has some random articles written twice. The first one is using easy words, while the second one expresses the same idea using more difficult vocabulary. The content of both are identical. I hope you find them useful.

Those who are not true beginners may skip Part I. They may find it too easy.

Some may feel that the topics are not in any logical order. Conversation is not bound by too many rules. By its nature it is free and unscripted. This text makes it easy for learners to go to any topic they like and to apply what they learn to other topics.

Have fun doing so.

I welcome feedback from students and teachers.

Peter D. Ward

Lesson One: Pronunciation:

To make English sounds easy to learn, usually just two pronunciations for each vowel will be given. Very few exceptions will be mentioned; learning all the exceptions would cause brain sprain or give students a headache.

Long and short vowels:

You will notice that the short 'a' sounds like 'ah' while the long 'a' sounds like its name 'ay'. The short 'e' sounds like 'eh'; the long 'e' sounds like the way the letter 'e' sounds. The short 'i' is pronounced 'ih'; the long 'i' is pronounced "I" or 'eye'. The short 'o' is pronounced 'auh', while the long 'o' is pronounced like the letter 'o'. The short 'u' sounds like 'uh'; the long 'u' sounds like 'u' or 'you'. Note that the final 'e ' in most words is silent. (It has no sound at all.)

Mat mate; pet Pete; sit site; not note; cut cute.
Pat pate; met mete; bit bite; dot dote; mutt mute.
Sat sate; men mean; kit kite; lob lobe; dun dune.
Bat bate; den dean; rip ripe; rob robe; tub tube
Tap tape; ten teen; sin sine; con cone; mull mule
Cap cape; wed weed; twin twine; cod code; us use, Sam same
fed feed; slid slide; hop hope; cur cure
Can cane; bed bead; din dine; ton tone; cub cube
Fat fate; set seat; tin tine; tot tote; Jun June
Van vane; led lead; pin pine; rod rode; jut jute

Diphthongs: (Two vowels together)

'Ea' is pronounced like a long E. The 'a' has no sound. E g.: fear, near, gear, dear, weak, wreak, beat, ear, eat, hear sear, peat, feat, seat, clear, heat, meat, neat, wheat, ease, smear, rear, please, flea, teat, shear, Michael, weasel, tear (-crying), year, clear, shear, spear, and many others.

However, in some -ea words –ea is pronounced like a long 'A'. Bear, great, tear (rip), wear, swear, pear, are the most common. (In the word 'create' both the 'e' and 'a' are pronounced separately.) Note that some words with 'ei' are also pronounced like '-ay'. E.g. weigh ("way"), sleigh ("slay"), neighbor, deign, feign, reign, rein, freight, and lei. (In the word 'height '- the 'e' has no sound.)

In –oa words the 'a' is silent. E.g: coat, goat, boat, moat, float, gloat, stoat. In the words: walk, talk, folk, and yolk the 'l' is silent. In the words listen, glisten, and often, the 't' is not pronounced. In though, dough, through (tho', do, thru') the 'gh' is not pronounced. In rough, cough, slough, tough – the –'gh' is pronounced like an 'f'. In 'kn' words such as knock, knit, know, knack, knot, knuckle, and many others, the 'k' is silent. 'Ph' is pronounced like an 'f'. E.g. phone, phonetics, photo, philosophy, philately, philander, philanthropist, phenomenon, phial, Philip, Philippines, phishing, sophist, atrophy, and many others.

In words that end in –mb, the final 'b' is silent. Comb, thumb, numb, lamb, climb, dumb, plumb, limb, bomb, womb, succumb, and tomb are the most common.

A few words end in –mn but the final 'n' is not pronounced. E.g. autumn,   condemn, contemn, column, limn, and solemn are the most common.

Sometimes words are pronounced the same even though the spelling is different. The following are some examples, but there are many other words that could be included. Tee tea, bow bough, berry bury, meet meat, weak week, rain reign rein, so sow sew, fair fare, steel steal, sleigh slay, see sea, do (music note) dough, reed read, red read, close clothes, sum some, steak stake, pain pane, Dane deign, fane feign, faint feint, sent cent scent, seen scene, seer sear, soar sore, flour flower, sine sign, hair hare, beer bier, peer pier, plum plumb, pair pear, know no, knew new, root route, feat feet, great grate, road rode, peace piece, cereal serial, mail male, none nun, wring ring, write, right, herd heard, etc.

Occasionally some words that are spelled the same have different pronunciations and different meanings. E.g. polish Polish, record record, bow bow, row row, minute minute, intimate intimate, read read.

For some students, the difference between R and L is not easily perceived. The following exercise with a native speaker will prove useful. It may help non-native speakers to pronounce the "R" as if it the word began with "oorrr", curling the tongue back in the shape of a "C" before moving it forward.

Raw	Law	Rap	Lap
Red	Led	Rex	Lex
Rice	Lice	Right	Light
Row	Low	Rob	Lob
Rush	Lush	Rug	Lug

Word Linkage:
Make the distinctions in the following list, but make them while linking the words in the manner of continuous within-phrase articulation. (Use them in a short sentence.)

The arm aid – They are made
We may cry – We make rye
Let's find Danny --Let's find Annie
Do it with ease- Do it with these
We may drum - We made rum
I see a gray train – I see a great rain
I said: "ill eagle" - I said: "illegal"

She's elected – She's selected
It is his swill – It is his will
In each ear – In each cheer. In each year
With fisher ease - With fisheries
It was a great trade – It was a great raid
What great loves – What gray gloves
My recent mail – my re-sent mail
Teacher More – Teach her more
Do well here - Dwell here
He's friendly – He's friend Lee
It's bar noise – It's barn noise
I'll sue them – I'll soothe them
See much -   Seem much
It's cash owed   - It's cash showed
Steep rice – Steep price
A car nation - a carnation
Look lean – Look clean
How sad   -House ad
Let's kill – Let skill
Ventilator - vent till later
God bless – godless
It's so prim   ---------   It's soap rim
That's all foreign-   That's all Forin
He's dancing with delight.........He's dancing with the light .
He's a nice man - he's an ice man
I hear the roar- I hear the rower
He said "I'll see–   He said " aisle C"
Was the bar made hot? Was the barmaid hot?
Sell her soup -   cellar soup
I see them mending the fence.- I see them ending defense.
Move the right light. –Move the light right.

How To Use This Text:
This text book begins with the indefinite and definite article. If a student does not understand the explanation, the examples will help to make it clear. It includes a simple test to check comprehension. Greetings, introductions, and some useful sentences follow. Then prepositions in short sentences make it easier for students to understand. After that verbs are reviewed. This section includes present, past, and future, as well as how to make questions and use helping verbs (modals). Some example conversations are offered so students can see how verbs are used. Next adjectives or pronouns dealing with quantity are given with many examples, and also a self-administered test is available to check comprehension.

The first part of the text can be a review for those who are not really beginners. (False beginners) Short stories or conversations are provided as examples only. Do not memorize them. Read or listen to the conversation. Note how each sentence is connected to the other sentences.

Topics are extended by giving a reason, talking about an experience, providing a time frame, saying the same idea in other words, showing feelings related to the topic, possible results, giving advice or a comment, expressing cause and effect, mentioning aspects of the topic, or even asking a question.

Conversation should not be limited to questions and answers. The speaker should provide some material for the listener. A question followed by a simple "yes" or "no" is not considered great conversation. Telling people what they already know is usually not interesting unless it is followed by an opinion, comment, or interpretation. E.g. Tokyo is a very big city. Japan has many train stations. Japanese people speak Japanese!

"Tokyo is very big city. I love to go shopping there," sounds much better than statements of fact. Also, do not be afraid to let the conversation flow into another different topic. Conversation is like a river, not a railroad. When beginning a conversation, to ask a question it is not always the most natural way. A comment before a question is a smoother way to start. For example: "I enjoy taking this train every day. How about you?

After each short conversation there is a brief analysis of what was said. Next we have pattern practice which is worth remembering. Finally, there are a few challenge topics where some learned patterns can be used. At the end of the book there are over one hundred topics listed. They have been selected because each one has two sides; speakers can choose to be for or against. Also, I have included some readings to improve vocabulary. Each article is written twice; the first one using easy words and the second one employing more difficult vocabulary. The topics cover a variety of experiences and commentary on many different issues.

As mentioned before, the order in which lessons are learned-especially for intermediate learners –is not important. Sentence patterns and thinking patterns are most important.

Definite & Indefinite Articles: The , A, An

The – used before nouns to mean one or many <u>specific</u> items, & for bodies of water. (Specific means – narrowed down to one.) **For example**: The sun, the moon, the earth, the windows, the people, the countries of the world; the sky, the students, the boss, the news, the end, the Pacific Ocean, the Atlantic, the Sumida river…

The – is used for usual (general) topics of conversation. **E.g**. the weather, the economy, the topic, the aim, the reason for, the score, the truth, the family, the cost of living, the exchange rate, the world, the news…

The –used before superlatives. **E.g**. the best, the biggest, the most expensive, the least important, the shortest, the oldest, the greatest, the worst, the tiniest.

The – used for one aspect of a topic. **E.g**. the top, the bottom, the color, the outside, the price, the shape, the inside, the front, the back, the left side, the area, the right side, the number, the distance, the beginning, the middle, the end, the center, the difference, the roof, the foundation, the labor, the extent, the weight, the length, the width, the height, the cost,..

The – used before plurals. **E.g**. Open the windows, look at the children, move the chairs, watch the ants, eat the apples, share the cookies, close the doors, the members of the team. The U.S.A. The U.N. The United Nations.

The- used when a relative clause is expressed or understood. **E.g**. Give me the pen which you have. Move the book which is on the table. Look at the blackboard (which is here). Return the pen (which I loaned you.) Look at the game (which is on now).

Listen to the teacher (who is here.) I am waiting for the bus (which is scheduled to come soon.)

But * -I am waiting for **a** bus – **any** bus that comes.
(In conversation, do not worry about using relative clauses. Instead of relative clauses, speakers often prefer two short sentences, E.g. I bought the pen which was on sale. = This pen was on sale. So I bought it. I found the pen which I had lost. = I lost my pen but then I found it.)

The – used to show order/placement. **E.g**. the first page, the last page, the second step, the last one, the 21st, the second of May, the prior owner, the previous day, the next page, the following night, the same day, …….

The - used for the second sentence about a previously mentioned subject or topic.**E.g**. I went to a store. The store was crowded.

THE- is seldom used before proper nouns.(The Hague, The United Kingdom are two exceptions). If proper nouns are used as adjectives , **The** <u>can </u>be used. **E.g**. The Tokyo Fire Dept. The Japan Weekly Newspaper. The Tokyo Dome. The Hiroshima Carp. The London Zoo. Etc.**The** is used before a noun in a typical sense. E.g. The <u>wheel</u> was a great invention. The phone has helped communication greatly. (This means all wheels/phones since their invention.
A – is used for one of many, <u>not specific</u>. **E.g**. Give me a pen. (Any pen). Buy a ball, take a rest, go for a walk, go on a trip, take a nap, give me a dollar, send him a message, give her a chance, don't buy a ticket, wait for a taxi.
An – is used instead of A before words beginning with a, e, i, o and sometimes u. **E.g**. an apple, an egg, an igloo, an orange, an umbrella, an ant, an elephant, an iguana, an octopus, an uncle,

But a uniform, a university, a unique color, a unicorn. (When 'u' is pronounced like 'YU' use A ; if 'u' sounds like "uh" use AN. **Note**: A one-man bus, a once in a lifetime chance, he's a European.)

When talking or writing about single letters of the alphabet, AN goes before: a, e, f, h, i, l, m, n, o, r, s, x. A is used before: b, c, d, g, j, k, p, q, t, u, v, w, y, z. **E.g**. Use an "f", an "l", an "o", a "u", and an "r" to spell 'flour.' Use a "c", an "h", an "a", and a "t" to spell 'chat'.

No A, AN, or THE : When making a general statement that is usually true, use the plural without "the". **E.g.** Cars are useful = all cars. Dogs chase rabbits. (Most dogs). Cats kill mice. People like vacations. (Most people.) Men and women like sports. Cell phones are handy. Mistakes are costly. Wars are cruel. Babies are cute. (All babies). Fish live in oceans. Dogs like people.

When talking about general topics, especially food, drink, & transport, there is <u>no</u> A or THE. **E.g**. I eat rice. She drinks tea. We buy bread. We have time. They need oil. We use paper. She sells fish. I burn coal. He craves attention. I came by taxi. He goes by train. He travels by plane. She likes cars. He takes photos of trains. We talked about comics.

*If the object is in a container or measured, then **a** is used. **E.g.** He wants a cup of tea. She buys a kilogram of rice. I burn a ton of coal. I need a liter of milk. She wants a meter of cloth. He has a fever of 38.9 C.

The Sentence to Remember: My mother is in **the** kitchen; we have **a** big kitchen. (Only one and one of many.)

Review of Definite & Indefinite Article: Insert :a, an, the or nothing.

1. She has _____ pen and _____ eraser.
2. _____ color of her pen is _____ blue.
3. Buy ____ comic and all _____ pens that are on _____ sale.
4. _____ captain hit _____ single and _____ home run.
5. ____ cats usually don't like ____ dogs.
6. How is ____ weather in ____ Hokkaido today?
7. _____ first page is ____ hardest.
8. ____ boss has ____ short temper.
9. ____ children like ____ games.
10. ____ best student asked ____ question. He is _____ only child.
11. There is ____ tax on ____ cigarettes.
12. ____ road to ____ bridge is blocked. Let's take ____ shortcut.
13. Do you have change for ____ dollar? Give me ____ four quarters.
14. I scored ____ only goal of ____ game in ____ last minute.
15. I have ____ friend who lives in ____ Tokyo.
16. Give me ____ hand with ____ homework.
17. ____ sun will shine in ____ little while.
18. ____ principal asked ____ teacher to call ____ police.
19. ____ poor will always need _____ help.
20. ____ students hate _____ tests.
21. She has ____ stamp with ____ rose on it.
22. This is one of _____ oldest books in ____ world.
23. ____ new student is ____ happy child.
24. Never tell ____ artist his painting is like ____ photo!
25. He tried to ask ____ teacher ____ difficult question.
26. _____ rich man has _____ home in Ginza and _____ second one in Izu.
27. Give me ____ hint about ____ puzzle no one can solve.
28. I have _____ umbrella that is _____ unique color.

29. ____women like shopping when there is _____sale on.
30. ____week after next, ____few students will have _____test.
31. He found _____ wallet on _____ train in _____Tokyo.
32. I will wear _____ uniform when I go to ____ high school.
33. _____wheel was _____ great invention.
34. This is one of ______ easiest tests ____ student can take!
35. ______ unicorn is _____ mythical animal.

Answers to : A, AN & THE cloze test. (x = blank)

1.a, an, 2. the, a 3. a, the, x,4. the, a, a, 5. x, x, 6. the, x,7. the, the, 8. the, 9. x, x, 10. the, a, an, 11. a, x, 12. the, the, a, 13. a, x, 14. the, the, the, 15. a, x, 16. a, x, 17. the, a, 18. the, a, the, 19.the, x, 20. x, x, 21. a, a, 22. the, the, 23. the, a, 24. an, a, 25.the, a, 26.the, a, a, 27. a, the, 28. an, a, 29. x, a, 30.the, a, a, 31. a, the, x, 32. a, x, 33. the, a, 34. the, a, 35. The, a.

Greetings:

A. Hello, how are you? B. I am very well, thank you. **OR**: B. I am fine thank you, and you? A. Couldn't be better. (I can't complain.)
A. Good morning, how are things? B. Just fine, and how are you?
C. Hi, how is it going? D. Just great, and how are things with you?
E. Hello, how is everything? F. Just fine. How is everything with you?
G. How are you doing? H. I am fine, and how are you?
I. Hi, you are looking well today. J. I feel fine thank you.

Alternative Greetings:
A. How are things with you?
B. Couldn't be better. How are you doing?
A. Can't complain. You're looking good.
B. I feel great. How is the family?
A. They are fine. Thanks for asking.
A. What's up?   B. Nothing much. How is life treating you?
 A. I am fine. Just the same old schedule.

Meeting for the First Time: Introductions:
In introductions, it is usually best to introduce the older person to the younger. Use the same level of formality for both people unless one is a family member.
"Mr. Jones, I'd like to introduce (you to) Ms. Smith." "Mr. Jones, I'd like you to meet my son Jack."

1. John, this is my friend Tom Jones. Tom, this is John Adams.
OR. John, I'd like to introduce you to Tom Jones. (Tom, I want you to meet John Adams.)
2. How do you do Mr. Jones? I am happy to meet you.
OR. How do you Mr. Adams. It's a pleasure to meet you.
OR. Please call me John. We are not so formal here.

1. Let me introduce you to Maria Endo, our manager. Maria, this is David Bell from London.
2. I am very pleased to meet you Ms. Endo. I was looking forward to meeting you. (I am very glad to make your acquaintance.)
3. I am very pleased to meet you Mr. Bell. Welcome to Tokyo.
Goodbye:
Well, I must be going now. It was a pleasure meeting you. Goodbye John. Goodbye, Tom. I am glad to have met you. Take care, I hope to see you again. Goodbye now.

Survival Emergency English:

If you are in danger (being attacked/robbed) in a place with many homes (a residential area), shout: "Fire, Fire," as loud and as often as you can. People often think "Help" is a joke, but everyone is afraid of fire. So people will come to find out where the fire is. When they come, you can ask for help.

One sentence to remember is: **There is something wrong with**…..
 It can be used in hospital: There is something wrong with my arm.
At the dentist's: There is something wrong with this tooth.
At the garage, There is something wrong with my car.
 At the jeweler's: There is something wrong with my watch.
When the repairman (plumber) comes: There is something wrong with the sink.
When the electrician arrives: There is something wrong with this switch.
 I need a police station. I just lost my handbag/wallet/credit card.

 I need a phone. I cannot find my passport. I must call my family.
 My important papers were stolen. I need to call my embassy.
 Do you have a first aid kit? My child is injured…bleeding...hurt.
 Does anyone here know CPR? This man has stopped breathing.

Call 110. (911)? Call an ambulance… the fire station… That house is on fire.   (Make sure you know the emergency phone number of the country in which you are staying. But be careful; in some third world countries, police like to get bribes. (money).

Please help me. My 4-year old son is lost. He is wearing blue clothes.
Is there a restroom (toilet) near here? Where is the (toilet) restroom?
Where is the ladies' room? Where is the men's room?
Is there a drinking fountain near here? My child is thirsty.
Where is the nearest drugstore? (pharmacy or chemist shop)

Prepositions:

A preposition is a word that shows position, direction, or time when something happens or happened. The following examples will help you to understand how prepositions are used.

The pen is **on** the table. The table is **near** the window. The window is **on the right side of** the door. The English book is **under** the magazine. The magazine is **on top of** the English book. There is a photo **of** Mt. Fuji **in** the magazine. The English book is **between** two Japanese books. The books are **beside** a dictionary.

Among my Japanese books there is one English book. Jon sits **in front of** the blackboard. **In the back of** the classroom there is a bookshelf. Jon's sister sits **behind** him. Her friend Jan sits **on the left side of** the classroom. They look **at** the clock **on** the wall. **At** home he sits **at** the table **opposite (facing)** his sister. The family sit **around** the table. They talk **to** each other **during** dinner. The light is **above** the table. The dog sits **on** the floor **behind** Jon.

Jon studies **in** his room **after** dinner. His sister Mary studies **before** dinner. They will go on a trip **on** the first Sunday **in** May. They will drive **from** Tokyo **to** Sendai.

They will stay **at** a small hotel. The hotel is **close to (near)** a large supermarket. Their cousin will meet them **in** Sendai **at** the hotel **at** 5:00 PM **on** Monday, May 5th. They may take a photo **of** an eagle flying **over** the hotel. They will walk **to** a restaurant.

While **in** Sendai, Jon will eat eggs **for** breakfast **for** three days **in** a row. He may buy a souvenir **for** his friend. He put socks **into** his suitcase. His grades are **below** average. We drove **along** a narrow road. A dog ran **across** the street. I like all fruit **except** lemons. He lives **beyond** the river. The boy went **down** the steps. The town was ruined **by** the typhoon. He took the cups **off** the table.

She ran **toward** her mother. Snow fell **throughout** the country. He is popular **within** his own country. She studied **until** midnight. I drink coffee **with** sugar but **without** cream. A stone came **through** the window. He quickly ran **past** me. The ball went **over** my head and **into** the goal. There is a cellar **beneath** the house. Once **upon** a time… The pipes are **underneath** the road.

NOTES:

Review of Verbs:

The following section is just a review of verbs. (For students who know verbs well, this section can be skipped.) In English, if we number subject, verb, and sometimes the object or complement 1-2-3-, then questions are always 2-1-3. E.g. He is cold. – 1-2-3. Is he cold? – 2-1-3.You can help me.-1-2-3. Can you help me? 2-1-3.They will eat. Will they eat? They are working. Are they working?

The Verb 'To Be':

The verb 'to be' means "=". E.g. 1+1 = 2. One plus one is two. Two is one plus one. My name is Jon. Jon is my name. **It is used in three ways**. E.g. I am cold. (I am 32.) I am a pitcher. I am reading. They are comics. He is a child. She is pretty. She is a teacher. He is a pitcher. She is teaching. It is raining. They are drinking. *It is wet. It is a cap. We are hot. We are waiters. We are speaking. You are young. You are readers. You are reading. They are happy. They are batters. They are drinking milk. (*"It" is used instead of a repeating a noun, for weather, time, or a day of the week, temperature, or to point to an action following 'it. E.g. I have a **pen. It** is blue. It is cold today. It is now 5:30. It is Sunday today. It is now 35.2C. It is dangerous to catch a snake. It is easy to buy comics.)

The simple present shows that an action or feeling often happens, is repeated, is habitual, or states a fact or a belief. It is easily understood when adverbs are added. For example: I **usually** play tennis. He **never** comes late. She **seldom** goes skating. They **always** eat rice. We **sometimes** buy grapes. They **often** drink tea. I play tennis. She loves tennis. You like soccer. They eat apples. He goes shopping. We buy comics. The pen writes. The bees sting.

(Remember that the **simple present** has two forms: **Present**: play- do play; plays – does play.)

"Do play or 'does play'- when used in an affirmative sentence (that is, a sentence without "not") shows that the verb is stressed or emphasized. It is not used very often in this way, but we use the strong form to make questions and negative sentences. The 2-1-3 question is made using the 'strong' emphatic form of the verb for the present and simple past. E.g. You do play – Do you play? She does play –Does she play? She (does) buy - Does she buy? You (do) buy. Do you buy? I do play tennis. She does play tennis. You do like soccer. They do eat apples. He does go shopping. This pen does write.

Negative Sentences ("do not" or "does not") are **not** strong sentences. This is the way to make a negative sentence.) (When you see an apostrophe 'between two letters, it means that one or more letters have been left out. For example: I'm –I am, I'll – I will, etc.) We do not buy comics. (We don't buy comics.) The pen does not write. (The pen doesn't write.) Jack does not drink juice. Jack does not like juice. They do not eat lemons. I do not play golf. She does not buy toys. Jack and Jill do not go bowling. My friend does not work. You do not play. (You don't play.) She does not play. (She doesn't play.) I do not play. (I don't play.)

The present continuous (progressive) tense means that the action is going on or continuing right now. It is made by using the verb 'to be' + the –ing part of a verb. (The present participle)* E.g. I am reading now. He is working now. My friend is cooking. They are playing now. The children are waiting. Sometimes the – ing form can mean some action is going on at this time, not just now at this moment.

E.g. He is building a new house now. (This means the building is happening every day.) She is reading all of Shakespeare's plays. (Every day she reads some of the plays.) They are living in Tokyo. (They live in Tokyo now.) The meaning of the verb makes it easy to understand.
*(The –ing part of the verb is also called a gerund and can function as a noun.)

Example of Present & Present Continuous:

The dog is white. Your cats are black. She is tired. I am late. They are drinking. We buy books. You are speaking. She watches TV. He is listening. We are cooking fish now. He is going to university now. He studies English. She is working in Tokyo. It is raining now. It rains a lot in July. He eats candy. She is eating an apple now. I am reading a book. I don't like comics. Jack is watching soccer. He does not like baseball. My sister is cooking dinner. She does not like fast food. The boys are playing outside. They do not like TV. They are listening to music. They like classical music. It is hot today. I am sweating. I don't like summer. You are driving and I am navigating.
The above sentence pattern is : 1-2-3.

Questions: 2-1-3 Pattern + Answers:

Is the dog white? Yes, it is. Are your cats gray? No, they are not. Is she tired? Yes, she is. Am I late? No, you are not. Are they drinking? Yes, they are. Are you speaking? No, I am not. Is he listening? Yes, he is. Are we waiting for a bus? No, we aren't. Do you play tennis? Yes, I do. (No, I do not.) (No, I don't.)* Does she play tennis? Yes, she does. (No, she doesn't.

Does he go shopping? Yes, he does. Do you go by train? No, I do not. Does the pen write? Yes, it does.. Do they like TV? What are you doing? Do you like music? Is it hot today?

Do you like summer? Does Jack drink water? Yes, he does. (No, he doesn't.) (<u>Note</u> : In the answer to the last question, **he** is used instead of Jack.) <u>Note*</u>: Do you play tennis? Yes, I play – is <u>not</u> correct. **NOTE**: The verb can be repeated if a new idea is added. For example: Do you play tennis? Yes, I play **lawn** tennis. (Yes, I play **clay court** tennis.) "Lawn" and "clay court" are new ideas not in the original question. E.g. Do you like cars? Yes, I like **sports** cars.

The present continuous (the present progressive tense) or the simple present plus a future word can be used to express the future. E.g. He is visiting us tomorrow. He goes to bed after dinner. I am visiting Kyoto next week. I begin work after Christmas. He comes to Tokyo next Sunday. I work from 5:00 AM tomorrow. I go home at 10:00 PM. The bats come out after dark. The mailman comes on Monday. The game is at 8:30 PM tonight.

Wh- Questions: Present Continuous & Present:

For Wh- questions we use: where, when, what, why, *who, and *which.
Wh- questions are made by putting a 'Wh-' word in front of a simple 2-1-3 question. For example: Do you go fishing? Where do you go fishing? When do you go fishing? Why do you go fishing? What do you catch? Who goes fishing with you?
*Who can be used like the other Wh- question words depending on the meaning of the verb. For example: Who do you meet? Who do you teach? Who do you play with? Who do we play against? Who do you want? (Or Whom do you want?)

These examples are correct, but when asking about who does the action of the verb, 'who' just replaces he/she/it from the 1-2-3- pattern sentences.

Examples will make this easy to understand. She eats rice. Who eats rice? She does…I do...We do…He does. (We do not ask "Who does she eat?") Who cooks for the boys? (NOT : Who cooks the boys?) The meaning of the verb will help you. Who needs a pencil? Who is pitching? Who is driving?

***Which can be followed by a noun or pronoun**.   E.g. Which book do you like? Which one do you want? Which car is the best? Which do you want, tea or coffee? (In this question 'drink' is understood.) Which color do you want? Which is colder in winter, Tokyo or Sapporo? In this question, 'city' or 'place' is understood. Which team will win the game? Which is bigger, Tokyo or Osaka?

What are you doing? I am doing my homework. (Homework) Who is she? She is my friend. (My friend.) Where are they working? In Tokyo. Why is she crying? Because she is sick. (To get attention.) When is she coming here? At 5 o'clock. Why is she drinking juice? She is thirsty. (It is hot.) A short answer is OK in conversation, but one can always add one or two more sentences.

What do you play? Tennis. (I play tennis.) Where do you play? In school. When does she play? After school. Why does he play soccer? Because he likes it. Who plays baseball? I do. (They do. He does. Jack does.) Why do you play soccer? It is my favorite sport. (Because I like it.)

Who is reading a book? Who likes comics? Who does not like comics? What is the name of the book? Is it interesting?

How many pages do you read every day? What is Jack doing? Does he like baseball? Who is cooking dinner? Why is she cooking dinner? Does she like eating out? Who is outside? What are they doing?

How come =Why. (How come – is **not** related in any way to the meaning of 'how' or 'come'.) 'How come'- can be first or last in a question. How come you don't play golf? **OR** : You don't play golf, how come? How come + 1-2-3 pattern, or, 1-2-3 + how come. It can be used with affirmative or negative sentences. E.g. How come you play golf? How come you like snakes? How come you don't like snakes? How come they are drinking now? How come you come by taxi? How come you don't drive here? She is always late, how come? How come there is no heat in this room? How come we can't park our car here? He won't join our soccer team, how come? How come you cannot help me?

*HAVE: this verb can be used in two ways. 1. Similar to other verbs: Do you have a pen? Does she have any books? 2. Like the verb 'To be': Have you a pen? Has she any books? Have you time to help me. I haven't any books.

CAN: Can is a helping verb. (Also called a modal or auxiliary verb.) This means that it is always together with a main verb. For example: You can speak English well. CAN means 1. To have ability, able to do something. E.g. I can ski. 2. It shows possibility or permission. E.g. You can wait here. 3. CAN- used in requests instead of 'may'. E.g. Can I use your phone please?

CAN is both present and/or future. E.g. I can help you now and tomorrow. We can play soccer if it stops raining. We can listen to music on the bus. You can go now.

CAN follows the same rules as other helping verbs. It is easy to use as it never changes. E.g. I can go, she can go, you can go, they can go. Can I go? Can she go? Can you go? Can they go? When can I go? Who can go? When can we go? Etc.

COULD: is the past of CAN. It shows ability in the past, a polite request, instead of 'can', or a suggestion. E.g. She could see Mt. Fuji from her apartment. I could not come last week. Could you drive me to the station? We could order pizza instead of cooking.

MAY:

Is a helping verb (modal/auxiliary) to show possibility, likelihood, to or ask permission. E.g. It may rain later. You may get wet. May I call a taxi for you? MIGHT is the past of 'may' and is often interchangeable with 'may'. It also expresses weak probability or possibility. E.g. You might try calling the police. She might have gotten lost. An earthquake might knock down our building.

Simple Past:

The simple past is used to report an action that took place in the past, i.e. at least one second ago, and the action is finished. The speaker wishes to tell listeners that something happened. When or where the action happened may or may not be mentioned. The simple past is formed by adding –ed (or –d if the verb ends in -e) to the simple present form of the verb. E.g. Paint –painted, cook- cooked, play –played, use- used. However, many English verbs do not follow this rule. E.g. go-went, eat-ate, drink- drank, grow-grew, speak-spoke, come-came, etc.

Similar to the present tense, the past has **two forms**: paint-**did paint-painted**; go-**did go-went**, eat-**did eat-ate**, speak-**did speak**– spoke. The 'did paint', 'did go' form is used for strong affirmative sentences. It makes the sentence or statement stronger or more emphatic. (The strong past or emphatic use of 'did' is seldom used.) For example, if a teacher tells a student "You didn't study!" The student may reply "I did study." We need 'did' for negative sentences, and to make questions, E.g. I (did) paint, you did not paint, did they paint? I did go, he did not go, did you go? (In the past tense, there is no 's' added for 'he, she, it, or name.) They did not play. (They didn't play.) He did not play. (He didn't play.) (If you forget the past of a verb, especially the irregular past, use the strong form of the verb. In such cases do not stress the word 'did'. E.g. I did go fishing. I did see a shark. "I went fishing, and I saw a shark" is better, but the above two 'did'- sentences are easily understood. If the speaker says: 'I go fishing yesterday'- it is impossible to understand.)

Negative: She did not play the guitar. We did not walk to school. You did not bake cookies. It did not snow. They did not buy pens. I did not study. (As in the case of the present, 'did not play' is not strong, it is just negative. It can be shortened to 'didn't'.)

Questions: 2-1-3 Pattern:

Did she play the violin? Yes, she did. (No, she did not.) Did you walk to school? Yes, I did. Did they watch TV? No, they did not. Did they wait for us? Yes, they did. Did you cook a tasty meal? No, I didn't. Did Mary want a car? Yes, she did.

Did she go home? Yes, she did. (No, she did not.) Did you come here by taxi? Yes, I did. Did they buy comics? Did he see a movie? Did Mary eat apples? Did you drink milk?

Wh- Where did she go? Home. (She went home.) What did she play? The violin. (She played the violin.) When did they buy comics? Yesterday. (She bought them yesterday.) What did he see? A movie. (He saw a movie.) (Why did she make cookies?Because her family likes them. How come she drank milk? She likes it. (She had no water.) How did they play? They played well…badly… poorly...fast. Who went? I did...she did…we did…Jon did. Which store did you go to? The one near my home. Which one of those books did you read? The green one. How did you come here? By taxi. How did Jon play? He played well. How many goals did he score? Two.

Past & Past Continuous:

The past continuous sometimes called the past progressive) shows that the action happened in the past and hints that it took time. E.g. I was painting my home yesterday. We were swimming. They were reading books.

It is also used when an action that was happening is interrupted by another action. E.g. I was eating lunch when the phone rang. He was jogging when a dog bit him. One action is in the simple past. The order of the sentences can be reversed (changed). E.g. When the phone rang I was eating lunch. A dog bit him when he was jogging.

The past continuous is used when two actions are going on at the same time. E.g. She was driving while her baby was sleeping. I was studying while you were reading comics. She was listening to the radio while she was driving. (The subject can be the same for each sentence or different.)

It can also be used when we add the time when the action was happening. E.g. I was living in Boston for two years. This morning we were playing golf. I was reading a book yesterday. (I don't like comics.) Jack was watching soccer on TV. He did not watch baseball. My sister was cooking. They did not watch TV. You were listening to classical music. The radio was on. It was hot yesterday. I was sweating. I was enjoying vacation when the boss phoned me. I was going to the station when I met an old friend. When he fell he broke his arm.

More, most, less, least, some, many, any, much, few, enough, plenty.

These words are adjectives (and sometimes pronouns).They deal with quantity and amount. The following examples will help you to remember that 'any' is usually used for questions and negatives. 'Many' and 'few' are used for countable quantity. 'Much' and 'less' are used for non-countable quantity.

'Some' can be used for an unspecified number or quantity. 'Less' and 'more' are comparative adjectives of quantity. "A lot of " can be used for count or non- count nouns. E.g. I have a lot of water. She has a lot of books.

The following example conversation will show you how to use these words.

Examples:

1.Do you have any paper? I need some to finish my homework. Just a few sheets will be enough.

2. Sorry, I don't have any. (I have no paper.) (I have none.) Why don't you ask Jon? I know he has some. He always has the most paper.

1. I need to add a few more colors. Do you have any green paint?
I won't use much. I have plenty of red and yellow. I think I used too much green.

2. I have a little left in this container. You may use all of it. I have more at home. I always use less paint than you. You use more than anyone. You don't need to use so much. Jack uses too much blue - his favorite color.

1.The teacher advised us to use less paint this time. But when I don't have much time, I usually use too much paint. I know I use too many colors.

2. Your project will look like a rainbow. Mine will look like a fence! I hope six pages will be enough. Now I have to make up a story to go along with my masterpiece. The teacher wants us to be a combination of Shakespeare and Michelangelo.

1. You should have no trouble. You are always reading comics, and you have a good imagination. Can you give me a few ideas for a story?

Review Quiz:
Circle one word in each sentence: many, most, much, any, some, no, little, less, least, few, plenty, enough, fewest, none- in the following review page.

1.Do you have any/some candy? I want any/some.
2.She went shopping. Now she has any/no money left.
3.I need some/any/few paper. I don't have some/any/none.
4.Do we have any/plenty/many time to eat a snack?
5.Do you have some/any/few brothers?
6.I have plenty/many of rice. Do you want some/many more?
7.She has many/much pencils. I have only a many/few.
8.He eats too many/much rice. He should eat less/little.
9.We have only a less/little water. We need more/much.
10.They want less/more homework. They get too much/many.
11.You have more/many pens than I; give me at less/least one.
12.Does she have any/few cookies? I want a few/much.
13.One sandwich is much/enough for me. I can't eat any more/much.
14.Buy much/any/more rice. We don't have any/some left.
15.I eat more/least/ little than you. My father eats the much/most/less.
16.Let's play for a few/some/many minutes. We have many/some time.
17.We have plenty/many of stamps. Write at few/least one letter.
18.I don't have many/much money. Please lend me a some/few dollars.
19.She went to Kyoto a few/much/plenty times.
20.There are less/fewer boys than girls in that class.
21.Ten hours is enough/plenty time to go to Japan.
22.He has no/any time to study. He is busy working.
23.He has no more/many comics.
24.Do you want some/any candy? Try a piece; it is tasty.

25.He has the more/most pens. I have the least/fewest.
26.We have much/plenty of time.
27.Let's take a little/less rest before we go swimming.
28.One mistake is one too much/many. Zero defects!
29.She has many/plenty friends in Tokyo.
30.I'm broke. Please lend me any/little/some money.
31.She has no/any/few pets. She is allergic to fur.

Answers: 1. any … some. 2. no… 3.some …any. 4.any . 5. any. 6.plenty …some. 7. many … a few. 8. much… less. 9.little … more. 10. less… much. 11. more … at least. 12. any… few. 13. enough…any more.14. more …any. 15. more …the most. 16. a few …some. 17. plenty of… at least. 18. much… a few. 19. a few … 20. fewer… 21. enough… 22.no… 23. more… 24. Some… 25. the most… fewest. 26. plenty… 27. little… 28.many… 29.many… 30.some… 31.no…

Present Future

This is Jack; he is not tired. He is painting his room. I am good at painting. I usually help him. I am not tired today. I do not need a nap. John and Bill are helping him too. Jack does not like painting. (He does not like to paint.) He usually paints very slowly. I can help him before I go home. Then later, we will all go bowling. So we have a busy day ahead. Let's get started. I want to paint the doors and windows. They are hard to paint. Bill can paint the ceiling; he is tall. Let Jack mix the paint. He is not good at painting. (He is not much of a painter.) Let's start now.

Analysis of the above paragraph:

The paragraph tells us **what Jack is doing**. It mentions why he has people helping him. The speaker is a good painter. It tells us who paints what and why.

Pattern Practice:

Good at – can do well. She is good at dancing. I am not good at skating. They are good at tennis.-(They are good at playing tennis.)
Hard to paint # easy to paint. Japanese is hard to write. That car is easy to drive. Instant ramen is easy to make. Sushi is hard to make.
He's not much of a painter – He's not good at painting. I'm not much of a pitcher. She is not much of a singer. You are not much of a shopper. (Only used in the negative.)

Challenge :

a."Jon is tired now." (You can explain why he is tired, what he is going to do, what he is not going to do, how he feels, what he cannot do, what he wants to do, and you can comment on how he looks/sounds .

b."Jon and I are running a marathon, but Bill is going to win the race." (Explain why we will not win, or give reasons why Bill is going to win. –faster...more experience...younger...better trained...used to this course.. former Olympic runner.. .
c. I am sleepy today. (Explain why, what happened, what you are going to do. etc

Past:

Yesterday, Jack was not tired. He was painting his room. I decided to help him. I did not need a nap. John and Bill were helping too. Jack did not like painting. (He did not like to paint.) He painted very slowly. Jack was not good at painting. I helped him before his friends came. After painting, we all wanted to go bowling. So we were busy. (We had a busy day ahead of us.) I wanted to get started right away. I wanted to paint the doors and windows. They were hard to paint. Bill could paint the ceiling. (He is very tall.) We let Jack mix the paint. We all wanted to start so that we could finish quickly and go bowling.

Analysis of the above:

The above paragraph tells us **what the people were doing**. The tall person was the one painting the ceiling. We understand the reason why they wanted to start right away. It tells us what they wanted to do after painting. It also tells us why Jack was mixing paint.

Challenge:

a. Her sister Jane helped her. (How, what she did, why she helped, where, etc.)

b. The meal was a great success. (Why? How many ate it? What did she cook? What did they say? etc.)

c. My family did not go out to eat. (How come, what happened, who decided, what they did instead, etc.)

Future:

Tomorrow Jack will not be tired. He is going to paint his room. (He will paint his room.) I don't need a nap so I will help him. Jack may paint very slowly. (Jack intends to paint slowly.) I will help him before I go home. After painting, we are going to go bowling. We have a busy day ahead of us. I want to start now. I will paint the doors and windows. They will be difficult to paint. Bill is going to paint the ceiling because he is tall. (…as he is tall.) Jack is going to mix the paint. We want to start right away.

Analysis of the Above:

Jack is going to get help to paint his room. Bill is going to paint the ceiling. I am going to paint the doors and windows. We will be busy, but when we finish we are going to go bowling. Jack is not so good at painting so he will mix the paint.

Challenge:

a. Jack is going to fix his car. (What's wrong, why, where, when, how much, etc.)
b. Bill is going to help him. (Who is Bill? Why will he help? How long will it take? How come Bill and Jack are friends? etc.)
c. Jon will be there but he will not help much. (Why? How old is Jon?)

Questions: About a book

What were you doing? Who was reading? What were you reading? Did you read a comic? Where did you get the book? How come you did not read a comic? What kind of book were you reading? How many pages did you read? Did you finish reading it? Who wrote the book? Was it expensive? May I borrow it later? Can you lend it to me? Was the story made into a movie? Did you buy the book in Japan? Did you find it interesting?

About Jack watching sports on TV

What was Jack doing? What sport was he watching? What channel was it on? Did he enjoy the game? Did his favorite team win? When did he watch the game? How long did it take? When did he watch it? Was it an exciting game? Did Jack bet on the game? Did he ever play soccer? Was he good at it? Did he videotape (record) the game? How come he didn't watch baseball?

Someone cooked dinner

Who cooked dinner? What did he/she cook for dinner? Was it tasty (delicious)? How many ate dinner? How come you didn't order pizza? When did she start cooking? How come you didn't invite me to dinner? When did you eat? Why did she cook? Was your mother sick? Did you wash the dishes after the meal?

The weather

How was the weather yesterday? Was it cool? What did you wear? Were people sweating? Did you put on sunscreen? Did you get a tan? Did it rain? Did you use a parasol? Did you watch the weather forecast on TV?

Future:

1. I will read a book tomorrow. I am going to read a magazine tonight. I want to read two books next month. I hope to read all of them. My sister intends to read a book too. She expects to finish it in a month. I hope it will be interesting. We will discuss the books then. We can read every day after dinner.

2. Tomorrow, Jack is going to watch soccer on TV. He will watch English soccer. He is not going to watch baseball. He intends to watch at least two games. He hopes his favorite team will win. I may watch one game with him.

3. At 6 o'clock my sister will be cooking dinner. She will cook fish, rice, and vegetables. She will not go out to eat. She is going to cook instead of my mother. She hopes to surprise us with a special dessert. I am looking forward to dinner. I can't wait to see what is for dessert.

4. The boys will play outside. They are going to play for one hour. Then they may get tired. They do not intend to watch TV. They will play soccer. Most of them can play baseball, but they prefer soccer. Their parents are going to videotape the soccer game. It will be fun to watch it. They may sweat a lot. They will have to drink a lot of water. According to the forecast, it will be very hot in the afternoon.

Analysis:

1. This paragraph tells about what my sister and I will read.
2. This tells about Jack and his love for soccer.
3. This is about my sister's cooking.
4. This one is about boys playing outside in hot weather.

Challenge:
a. My brother is going to learn karate.
b. My sister is going to climb Mt. Fuji.
c. My father's new hobby is carpentry.

In answering questions, it is a good idea to say more than one word. This provides material for conversation and it can lead into other topics. E.g. "You are a fast runner. Do you play any sports? " Yes, I do. I play soccer every week. It is just a group of friends. We are not very good but we like to play."

Questions:

1..What will you read tomorrow? What kind of book are you going to read? How long will it take to finish it? Who else is going to read a book? When can you read?

2. Who is going to watch soccer? How come he does not watch baseball? How many games will he watch?

3. Who is going to cook instead of your mother? Do you know what we are going to have for dessert? What is she going to cook? 4. Who is going to play outside? How long will he/they play? Who will videotape the children? What will the weather be like tomorrow? If it is hot, what are you going to drink?

More Questions:

What are you reading? How many books do you read every month? Why don't you like comics? How come you don't like comics? Where do you get books? When do you read? How long do you spend reading? What kind of books do you like? Who is Jack? What is he doing? Where is he watching TV?

Which team does he like? Why doesn't he like baseball? Does he play soccer? Is he good at soccer? (Can he play soccer well?) (Is he a good soccer player?) When does your sister cook dinner? What is she cooking? Can she cook well? What is for dinner? How come she doesn't order pizza? Who likes eating out? What are the boys playing? Where are they playing? How come they are not playing inside?

How many boys are playing? Can I play with them? Why do you listen to music? What kind of music do you like? Do you have many DVD's? Where do you buy them? How hot is it now? Is everyone sweating? How come you don't like summer? How come you prefer winter?

MUST (HAVE TO V.):

Must' is a helping verb that is either present or future. 1. It is used to express obligation, command, or inevitability. E.g. I must pay my taxes. She must take a driving test. We all must eat and sleep daily.

2. 'Must' is used to show strong desire or strong recommendation. E.g. You must see that movie. I must go to the soccer game tonight. I must get to that bargain sale. You must try some of my freshly baked cookies. You must take a break now.

3. **'Must ' is used to express presumptive certainty or probability**. E.g. You must be hungry. (You had no lunch.) He has three new cars. He must be rich. She always gets 100 in all her tests. She must be very clever.

4. **Negative 'must' shows command or prohibition**. E.g. You must not smoke in church. You must not stick your chopsticks in the rice. You must not eat before your medical test.

5. **'Must' as a noun means a necessity**. E.g. In winter, warm clothes are a must. If you go to Japan, visiting Kyoto is a must.

Note: Must is stronger than 'should' or 'ought'. 'Must not v.'-obligation; but 'don't have to v.'- it is not required. E.g. You must not smoke on the plane. You don't have to go to the bank; you can use an ATM.

'Must' has no past, so the past of 'have to v.' is used. E.g. It was snowing so I had to drive slowly. I had to finish the story before I went to bed.

Would...Could...Should: Would is used to express a condition after 'if'. Usually the action is unlikely to happen or impossible. E.g. If I went to Mars I would bring back red rocks. If I could teach you Spanish, I would (teach you).

Would is used to show future intention expressed in the past. E.g. She told me she would phone me. He promised that he would come to my party.

Would can be used to show habitual action in the past. E.g. Grandma would tell me stories about her childhood. I would sit on her knee.

'Would like' is a polite way of expressing 'want'. E.g. I would like that book. Would you like a cup of tea ? (Polite) I would prefer coffee.

Could is used as the past of 'can', and instead of 'can' for polite requests. E.g. She could not come yesterday. Could you pass me the salt please?

Could is used to express possibility. E.g. They could be stuck in traffic now. You could be nice to your little brother for a change.

'Should' is used to express obligation, advice, or likelihood. E.g. You should drive slowly in a school zone. He should see a doctor if the pain gets worse. They should be here by now. It should be a good soccer game.

Could have...Should have ...

Both show possibility, missed opportunity, or comment after the fact. E.g. You could have phoned when you were caught in traffic. You should have the office number on your cell phone. (=You did not phone, and you do not have the office number on your mobile phone.) You should have passed the ball. We could have scored another goal. (= You did not pass the ball so we did not score a goal.)

Mini Conversation:

1. I forgot to buy a present for my mother's birthday. She must think I am an ungrateful child. I thought about it a few days ago but then it slipped my mind. (I forgot about it later.)

2. You could have sent her an email. You should have gotten her a gift card. You could have sent it from your I-phone. But there is still time. Better late than never. You should send her a gift special delivery. It would get there today.

1. Could I borrow your phone? I can't find mine. I could have left it at work.

2. Sure, here you are. When you are finished could you turn it off? My battery is low. I would charge it if I could, but my charger is in my wife's car.

Would have...is used to express one's feelings or imagined outcome about a condition that was not fulfilled. The conditional sentence (protasis) is in the past perfect tense.

E.g. If you had gone to Kyoto you would have enjoyed it. The patient would have recovered if he had seen a doctor earlier. The game would have been played if there had been no earthquake. The student would have passed the test if she had studied. If she had asked me I would have helped her.

Review Tenses: Insert one word in each blank: am, is, are, was, were, do, does, did, can, may, will, could, would, should, must. (Some questions can have more than one correct answer.)

1. He is very sick; he _________ go to the doctor. (see a doctor.)
2. The books_______ very difficult; the child ______ not read them.
3.Tonight I ______ free; I ______ going to watch TV.
4._____ you busy last night? I _____ going to phone you but I ____ n't.
5._______ you like tea or coffee? Sorry, I _____ n't drink either one.
6. There ______ a sale on. You______ go shopping with me.
7. She _____ not sleep at all last night; she _______ be sleepy now.
8. She ______ not like rats. She ________not have one as a pet.
9. The lawyer ______ read the will when the funeral ____ over.
10. They ________ phone you but they _____not know your number.
11. She _______speak two languages; she _____bilingual.
12. Next year I _______ go to Hawaii; it depends on my work schedule.
13. _______you please close the windows? It _______ cold in this room.
14. _______ anyone see my pen? It ______ on the desk five minutes ago.
15. If she had time she ________ help us. She _____ very kind.
16. Yesterday ______ cloudy. We ________ not see Mt. Fuji from here.

17. You _________ study very hard. The test ______ be very difficult.
18.If you _______ not pass this test you _________not graduate from school.
19. He _______ disappointed last night; his favorite team _______ not win.
20. She _________ be late for work tomorrow; there _______ so much snow.
21. I _________ see that movie! My favorite actress _____ in it.
22. She _________tell us if our work schedule _______ changed.
23. From the top of Tokyo Tower I _______ see Ueno Station.
24. They _______ not do homework so their teacher _______not happy.
25. We _______ going to go hiking if the weather _______ fine.
26. He _________ be happy if he _________ marry a princess.
27. I ______ tired because I _______ working hard and I _______ not take a rest.
28. She _________ a lot of exercise, and she _______ able to lose weight.
29. His parents _________ give him some advice; he______ still very young.
30. "Teach me Korean". " I __________ if I _________ but I_______ n't."
31. It _______ rain tomorrow so I _________ take an umbrella.
32. There _________ a few people waiting for the bus last night.
33. There _________ no mistakes in this sentence.

Review Tenses: There are other possible answers not listed here.

1. should…must...will. 2. are…can. 3. Am…am. 4. were…was…could/did. 5. would…do. 6. Is…should/can 7. did…may. 8. does…does. 9.will/can…is.10. would…did. 11.can…is. 12. may/should. 13. could…is. 14. Did…was. 15. would/could…is. 16. was…could. 17. must… will/may. 18.do…can/will 19. was…did. 20. will/may…is. 21. must/should… is. 22. should/would…is. 23. could. 24. did…was. 25. are…is. 26. will/would… can/could. 27. am…was…did/could. 28. did…was 29. should/will…is. 30. would…could…can   (can't).31.may…should/will/must 32.were. 33. are.

Tenses in Action:

Jack usually plays golf on weekends. Yesterday he was playing a round of golf with his wife. They played 18 holes before lunch. His wife got a hole in one. Jack was trying to beat her. However, he hit his ball into the water. He lost patience and his golf game got worse. But he will get over it. He should control his temper. (He has a short fuse. = He gets angry easily.) If he continues to get angry, his golf game will not get better. Now he must buy a few more golf balls. If he does not cool down, he may lose the next time too. I believe he is going to take some lessons from the local golf pro. That should help his game. I could help him control his temper, but he thinks he doesn't have a problem.

Analysis :
Jack competitive spirit gets him in trouble, and it does not help his golf game. The challenge is to get him to admit he has a problem.

Pattern Practice:

Get over- overcome, get better, recover,
I got over my cold in a few days. He will never get over his wife's death.
Lose patience- get angry, become impatient,
He lost his patience with the slow waiter. I lose my patience when I am asked rude questions.
Cool down- become calm. Be patient.
Please cool down; he made only a very small mistake.
(Cool down also means to recover after exercise or sports.)

Challenge:

Try to repeat the above story about Jack in your own words.
Make up a conversation & comments on the following:
a. Jon lost his credit card but he did not tell anyone.
b. Mary suddenly decided to visit her cousin who was not home.
c. Jack saw an accident on the highway but he kept on driving.

NOTES:

Why We Have A Paragraph Here:

The following section includes a paragraph which students can read. It gives them a chance to remember the main points of what is said or read. Students should learn how to summarize or remember the main points of the paragraph in their own words. Then comments can be added or questions asked about the content. They are all open questions, and the one answering can add one or two more sentences. This will make conversation easier to continue. One question followed by one short answer does not make a great conversation. Students should know the difference between English and English conversation.

For more advanced students, 'answering' the questions before they are asked can make their conversation much more interesting. It just means imagining possible 'Wh-questions and giving the information before one is asked.

The Paragraph:

Mary, 29, is Jane's friend. She lives in Hanno. Every Saturday in August she goes to Ginza in Tokyo by train to buy expensive cookies for her friends in Hanno. She spends three hours shopping and spends 20,000 yen. The train trip takes one hour. Even though there are many good stores in Hanno, she prefers Ginza.

Questions:

Who is Mary? How old is she? (What age is she?) Whose friend is she? Who is her friend? What is her friend's name? Where does Mary live? What does she like? Where does she go? Where does she go in Tokyo? When does she go to Tokyo? How does she go to Tokyo? How long does it take (to get there)? How does she go there? What does she buy? How many friends does she have? How long does she spend shopping? How much does she spend?

Where is Hanno? Do you know Mary? Is she your friend? Is she good at shopping? Does she have a lot of money? Is she rich? How come she buys expensive cookies? Why does she buy cookies? Why doesn't she buy fruit? Does she go shopping in July? Which is her favorite store? Will you go shopping with her? Can she go shopping in September? May I go with Mary? Was she shopping last Saturday? Is Mary married or single? When is her birthday? Will she go shopping next Saturday? Does she live near the station? Is Hanno near Tokyo? Does she go by express train or local train? How come she does not bake cookies? How about teaching her to bake cookies?

In conversation, a speaker can imagine these questions. Thus, he/she can expand the conversation easily without waiting for questions to be asked. Below are a few exaggerated **examples** of expanded conversations and exaggerated replies about the paragraph above.

Example # 1: You know Jane's friend Mary from Hanno. Let me tell you about Hanno. It is a small town in Saitama. It is not too far from Tokyo. It takes about an hour from Ikebukuro on the Seibu line. It is worth visiting, especially in spring and summer. They have a lot of interesting things going on. The way they celebrate the Doll Festival in March is unique.

Possible Reply:

I am afraid I don't know much about Saitama. I spent most of my life in Tokyo. My folks originally came from Kagoshima, so I always went there on vacation. But I hope to visit Hanno someday. I want to check out the Doll Festival. Remind me when it's March. I will definitely go.

Example # 2: I know an amazing young lady from Hanno. She is crazy about shopping. She has the time and money to do it. In August she spends her bonus on her friends. She has expensive tastes. She loves to surprise her friends with expensive presents. I don't understand how she does it.

Possible Reply:

That is amazing, especially now. Most people are trying to save money.
She must have a very good job. I'd love to meet her someday. Can I become one of her friends?

Example# 3: Some people take gift-giving too far. I know a lady in Hanno that thinks Ginza is the only place to go shopping. She goes there in August to buy gifts for her friends. I wonder how much she spends. It must cost her a lot. I wish I were one of her friends!

Possible Reply:

Some of my friends tell me you can get bargains in Ginza. However, I never found many. Maybe she knows someone in the stores there. Perhaps she gets a discount because she buys a lot. It wouldn't hurt to ask her. (You should ask her.)

Expecting 'Yes'

In conversation we make it easy for others by using questions that expect "yes", even though the answer can be "no". The same form is used to stress the obvious to begin a conversation. Examples will make this clear.

1. Don't you live in Tokyo? (OR: You live in Tokyo, don't you?) Didn't you go to school in Sendai? Wasn't my sister in your class? Won't you go to the class reunion next month? Wouldn't you like to meet her again? (You would like to meet her again, wouldn't you?)

2. Today is cold, isn't it? (Isn't it cold today?) That baby is cute, isn't she? Aren't those beautiful flowers? That table is heavy, isn't it?

For 1 above, the answer can be "no" (even though the speaker expects "yes".)

In # 2 the answer is always "yes" as the meaning is obvious (clear). #2 is used to begin a conversation – not to ask a question. It is considered to be small talk or a closed question. The only answer is 'yes". (The speaker knows the weather is cold…the baby is cute…etc. He/she wants to make it easy for the other person to answer, and possibly add one or two more sentences.)

If #1 is confusing or hard to answer, just ignore the "not" in the question. 'Don't you live in Tokyo' is the same question as 'Do you live in Tokyo?'

Expecting 'No':

Sometimes a speaker will ask a question where he/she expects 'no'. 'You don't like snakes, do you?' You are not American, are you?' 'Today isn't Friday, is it?' 'The deadline isn't tomorrow, is it?' 'You didn't meet my wife before, did you?' She won't come to the party, will she? You didn't drink all the tea, did you? She can't teach Chinese, can she?

The answer to these questions can be 'yes'. Think of the first question as: 'you don't like snakes, do you like snakes?'

No " No"; No "Yes"

Some questions cannot be answered with a simple 'yes' or 'no'. I hope the following examples will make it clear, but that depends on you.

1. I know you like rice. Do you eat it every day?

2. That depends. If we eat Japanese food we have rice. If we have Italian food we fix pasta.

1. You told me you buy rice in Hanno. How long does it take to go there?

2. It depends. If I drive it takes 30 minutes. If my brother drives it takes about 20 minutes. It also depends on the weather and the traffic. If it is raining, or if traffic is heavy, it takes longer.
1. You eat quite a variety of food at your home. May I ask what is for dinner tonight?

2. Don't waste your breath asking me. It depends on my wife. Or maybe it depends on what is in the refrigerator. I'm not particular about food.

1. You told me you don't snack while watching TV. Do you watch it every night?

2. It depends on what is on and whether it is worth watching or not. I don't like wasting time. Besides, I have to go to bed early. My kids depend on me to drive them to school every morning. Next year they will get their (drivers') licenses and be independent. I can't wait.

Analysis of the above:

The above questions cannot be answered by a simple "yes" or "no". 'Depends'- introduces a condition that may change the action, time, person, place, thing, travel, weather, price, etc. 'Depend' can also means to 'rely on'.(My kids <u>depend on</u> me to take them to school.)

Pattern Practice:

Depend – is determined or controlled by, is affected or changed by.
Depend – We depend on trains to travel in Japan. Skiing depends on how much snow there is. I depend on the Internet for news. How many apples I buy depends on the price. Overtime depends on my boss.
My studying depends on how I feel or when I get home.

Fix – to make or cook. She can fix breakfast in 10 minutes.

May I ask = Is it OK to ask? It may be impolite to ask but I'm asking.

Don't waste your breath- humorous way of saying "I don't know. "Or "don't ask me." "I cannot answer".

Particular about – hard to please, hard to satisfy.
My wife is particular about what she wears. He is particular about food.

Worth ….ing – has value, to do so is a good idea.
Kyoto is worth visiting. My watch is not worth fixing. This book is worth reading. The movie was worth going to. This pattern is worth remembering. The politician's speech wasn't worth listening to.

My kids will be independent. = They will not need me. July 4th, 1776, is the date America became independent. (It no longer relied on England.)

I can't wait = I am looking forward to it. I hope that time comes quickly.
I can't wait until payday. I can't wait to see your new car.

Challenge: Use 'depend' in all your answers to the three questions below.
 a. How will Japan get better?
 b. Will your sick friend get well soon?
 c. Where will you go on vacation?

The End of Part I

PART TWO

What happens when you do not know a word in English?
Maybe you stop speaking, keep trying to recall the word, ask
a friend, look it up in a dictionary, or feel guilty for not
studying harder.

What should you do when you forget a word? Relax, then
give the meaning of the word you cannot remember, or use
easy words to get your point across.

For example: I forgot or do not know the word "lost". So if
I cannot say: "I lost my pen", I can say the following: "I can't
find my pen. I had it earlier. It was on my desk. Now it is not
here. Did you see it anywhere? May I borrow one of
yours?"
Imagine you can't remember the English word "found".
What will you do? "This pen was on the floor. It is not mine.
Is it yours? Do you know the owner?" **OR** you can say:" I
picked this up. It is not my pen. Did anyone lose a pen? Who
owns this? "
Imagine you forgot the word 'late'. You could say: 'Class
started at 8:30. I arrived at 8:45. Sorry, I was not in time. (I
missed 15 minutes.)'

The important thing is that listeners understand what you
want to say. If they can understand **lost**, **found,** and **late**
without your mentioning them, that is great. Getting your
ideas into another's head is what is important; the words you
use are not. If you think you are going to learn all the English
words you will ever need in your lifetime, you will have to
study English forever!
Here are some words you can use to help you. Imagine you
do NOT know the words in bold type. Use other words or
sentences to make yourself understood.

"Words I Don't Know"

1. The table is **heavy.**
2. I buy **lottery tickets**.
3. I **moved** from Osaka to Tokyo.
4. I **forgot** my lunch.
5. I paid a **fine** for speeding.
6. I have a **reservation** for dinner at this café.
7. My friend is **sick**.
8. He needs a **hammer.**
9. Her **graduation** is next week.
10. The **population** of Tokyo is about 13 million.
11. She is very **wealthy.**
12. She teaches **origami.**
13. Japan has many **vending machines**.
14. She buys food in **local** stores.
15. The train was **crowded.**
16. Those stores are **convenient**.
17. His **hobby** is carpentry.
18. Kyoto is **famous**.
19. That driver was **drunk.**
20. That painting is an **original.**
21. I need Christmas **wrapping paper**.
22. Soccer is **popular** in Japan.
23. Someone **stole** my bike.

Answers to 'Words I Don't Know':

1. This table is not light. I can't move it. Please help me.
2. A ticket with a number on it. If it is picked, the ticket owner wins a lot of money.
3. I used to live in Osaka now I live in Tokyo. Let me give you my new address.
4. I don't have my lunch. I left it at home on the table. I'll have to buy lunch.
5. I have to pay money for breaking the law and driving too fast.
6. I phoned and asked you to keep a table for me. You promised me a table.
7. My friend is not well. He has to stay in bed. He has a fever.
8 . I need something heavy to hit this nail.
9. She is finished going to school. There will be a public ceremony, and she will get a special certificate to prove she has finished.
10. The number of people in Tokyo is about 13,000,000.
11 . She has more than enough money. She can easily buy what wants.
12. She teaches how to make animals and other shapes by folding paper.
13. You can buy things by putting money into a machine.
14. She buys food in shops near her home. She shops near her home.
15. There were many people on the train. I could not sit down. I had to stand.
16. These shops are near and they are always open. They are handy.

17. He spends his free time making things out of wood.
18. Kyoto is well-known all over the world. Everyone has heard of Kyoto.
19. The driver drank too much alcohol. He was not sober.
20. That painting is unique; it is not a copy.
21. I need pretty paper to put around Christmas presents.
22. Many people in Japan like soccer.
23. Someone took my bike, and he/she is keeping it.

TOPIC SELECTION: (Small Talk)

People usually talk about: what is present, the weather, the train/plane they are on, what happened just before their meeting, the newspaper headlines, the scenery, their travel (if one has traveled to get to the meeting place), cultural differences (if both come from different countries), upcoming holidays, food, sports, family, or seasons. (People usually avoid (do not talk about) religion or politics at their first meeting. It is not polite to ask questions about how rich someone is, the extent of his/her education, or marital status. It is not polite to ask women how old they are or if they are married or single.)

What is present: A Pen

1. That looks like a good pen. May I see it? Where did you get it?
2. I picked it up in a convenience store. It is not bad. It writes well and I like the color. I regret not buying two.
1. You are lucky. My pen is no good. Sometimes it does not write at all. I regret buying it. It was a waste of money.
2. In future why don't you buy a better pen? They don't cost that much, and you are not poor.
1. I know. I should buy more expensive pens, but I keep losing them. So I buy cheap ones. Then when I lose one I don't feel so bad.

2. Well, if you buy a good pen you will be more careful. You never lose that expensive phone you picked up for only $700.00 !

1. That's different. I usually buy only one phone every five or six years. No one keeps a pen that long. Besides, pens don't cost that much.

2. Your birthday is coming up soon, so why don't you drop a couple of hints. Maybe someone will give you a present of a pen.

1. That sounds like a good idea. I will try it. I hope it works. I do need a good pen.

Analysis:

The difference between a good and bad pen. Details on where the pen was bought, and why the owner likes it. Advice + reason. Reason for not buying a good pen. One possible way of getting a better pen.

Pattern Practice from the above:

It looks like a good pen. = Just looking at 'it', I think so. (If followed by an adjective – no 'like'. E.g. That book looks new. "Like" is followed by a noun. E.g. It looks like a new book. That looks like an expensive watch. That watch looks expensive. He looks like a strong man.

That man looks strong. That man looks like my uncle. (The last sentence means that 'that man' resembles my uncle- face, hair color, features, etc.

Get – pick up – purchase – synonyms for 'buy'.

When you go shopping, pick up a few apples; also, get a newspaper.

Regret – sorry for doing or not doing something. I regret going to the baseball game. (It was boring.) **OR** : I regret not going. (It was very interesting.) I regret eating so much ice cream. He regretted not going to the doctor. I regret not watching the movie. She regrets moving to Tokyo.

That sounds like a good idea. = When I hear it, I think it is a good idea. (Similar to 'looks' or 'looks like' above.) That sounds interesting. That sounds like a difficult job. That music sounds like Mozart. That sounds like interesting work. That work sounds difficult.

Besides- also, plus, as well. He has a cat and two dogs besides. Besides a Lexus, he has two German cars.

Drop a hint – hint at indirectly. Try to put an idea in someone's mind. He dropped a hint that he was interested in meeting my pretty cousin.

Challenge: Can you remember/repeat the
  conversation about pens. (In your own words.)
  a.   The Smartphone –easy/difficult to
       use.
  b. Baseball is more/less interesting than soccer.
  c. Karate/judo/aikido - pluses and
     minuses.

The Place You Are In:

1.This seems like a very nice part of the country. I think you are fortunate to be living here. Were you born here?

2. Actually I was born 500 miles from here. My father moved here to start his own business when I was only 5 or 6. So I grew up here and never left.

1.That was a good decision. You have everything here, the mountains, the ocean, and beautiful forests. The city is not so big, so it must be very pleasant all year round.

2. We have four very distinct seasons but winter does get very cold. Last winter it was below zero for the whole month of January. You are lucky you did not come then.

1. You're forgetting I am a Canadian and we have very cold winters too. But I think one can get used to them. I spent a couple of years in North Africa and the heat was terrible.

2. That must have been a great experience. May I ask what you were doing in North Africa?

Analysis:

One person likes the present location and is interested in how the other person came to live there. Cold is a common experience but one person did experience heat. So the conversation is ready to veer off in another direction- which is only natural! The conversation begins by talking about where they are and they will continue talking about Africa or some other topic.

Pattern Practice:

Seem – what one feels but not so strongly, give the impression.
This car seems to be new. I seem to remember meeting you before.
Distinct: different, separate,
Japanese and Chinese are distinct languages. Ford & GM are distinct car companies.
Must be – I think so, I bet,
He must be rich. You must be tired after working so hard.

Challenge:
      a.The car you have or rented vs. the one you wanted
      b. The best time to go to a vacation spot.
      c. The benefits/difficulties in speaking a second language.

What is present: The building where we are now.

A. This is certainly an unusual building. The shape and color are unique. How did you manage to get an office here? It must have been difficult.

B. Everyone comments on this place. It just happens that my brother-in-law was the architect who designed it. So you could say my marriage helped to get me an office here. I like it because it is quite central.

A. It is very convenient. The train station is just a five minute walk from here. My hotel is just around the corner. There are plenty of restaurants, and there is even a park nearby. It makes an ideal headquarters for an international company.

B. I am glad you like it. After our meeting we can spend a few minutes walking around the neighborhood. There are a few other buildings I would like to show you. Then we can decide on a restaurant for dinner. It's almost 9:00 o'clock, isn't it?

Analysis:
They talk about the unique aspects of the building and explain the family connection. One participant explains why he thinks it is convenient and gives information about the neighborhood.

Pattern Practice from the above:
Manage v.- to be able to do something even though it is difficult.(One meaning)
How did you manage to get this office? = Even though it was difficult, how did you get this office? How did you manage to carry all these parcels? How did she manage to get front row seats at the opera? How did he manage to meet the president? How does she manage to live on $100.00 a week?

It just happens =actually, luckily, (It just happened.) How did you get the movie star's autograph? It just happened I was painting her home. I just happened to park her car when I was working as a valet. It just happened we both went to the same high school. It just happens we are neighbors in LA.

We spend time …ing. We spent a few days skiing. She spent two hours shopping. She spends nine hours a night sleeping. They spend 12 hours a day working.*(She spends $200.00 a month <u>on</u> gasoline.) (We spend money **on** something we buy or do.) He spent $500.00 on skiing. Mrs. Marcos spent a lot of money on shoes.
Decide on- choose, pick, select. We must decide on a name for the baby. Let's decide on a color for the living room. He will decide on a menu later.

Challenge: Talk about the building you are in now.
        a. Two people talk about a painting on the wall.
        b. Two give their opinions about a new car they
          are viewing.
        c. Two discuss a beautiful flower arrangement.

The Weather:
A. The weather is much better than I had expected. I thought the city would be colder. I even brought a heavy overcoat and a sweater. What happened?

B. You came here at a very good time. The weather is getting nice and warm right now. Usually it is a little colder at this time of year. The cherry blossoms are just beginning to bloom, and spring flowers are everywhere. Perfect timing.

A. This is beautiful. The last thing I did before leaving home was shovel the driveway. We had a late spring snowfall. We should schedule all our meetings for this city and this season. I would vote for that.

B. But many people love the snow and winter sports. I love snow as long as I don't have to shovel it! However, I won't complain about this nice spring weather!

Analysis:
The weather he had expected; how he prepared for it.
Explaining why it is a good time to come here.
What he did before coming here. Why this place would be good for all meetings.
Winter

Pattern Practice:

Expected – imagined, thought, believed. The car was more expensive than I had expected. I did better on the test than I had expected. We expected to win.

As long as: since, because. As long as you are going to the post office, mail this card for me. As long as you're driving there, I'll go with you.

Complain about- to say one is unhappy with. People complain about the weather. Some complain about restaurant service. Students complain about teachers. Teachers complain about students. Grandma never complains about her grandchildren.

Challenge: Talk about today's weather.
  a.   Two people are complaining about hot/cold weather.
  b. The rainy season: two views.
  c. What two people think of the fall (autumn).

On the Plane:

A. We seem to be making good time. We may even arrive ahead of schedule. According to the airline we will arrive at 5:15 local time. Now it just 4:30 and we are almost there.

B. That's right. But we have a strong tail wind behind us. That makes everyone happy. A shorter flying time means less fuel used by the airplane. Do you have anyone meeting you?

A. My wife (husband) usually picks me up, but I often have to wait. Finding a parking space near the exit is not easy. I'll give her (him) a ring when we land. How about you?

B. I am just visiting on business. So I have to pick up a rental car and a good map. Maybe you can help me if you know some shortcuts through the city. I sometimes get on the wrong expressway (freeway). I am heading towards Orange County.

A. I'd love to help you but I have a very bad sense of direction. But I am sure the car rental people will help you.

Analysis:

1. Passengers are talking about the arrival time. They give a possible explanation for arriving ahead of schedule. One is being picked up by a spouse; the other passenger is on business and will rent a car.

Pattern Practice:
According to – as stated by, as announced by. According to the newspaper, there will be a bus strike tomorrow. According to my boss, this company expects everyone to quit smoking. According to the weather forecast, it will rain tomorrow.
Ahead of schedule – before we were supposed to arrive/finish. We finished painting the house two hours ahead of schedule. The built the new bridge a week ahead of schedule.
Give someone a ring – phone, call. Give me a ring if you can drop by tonight.

Challenge: Talk about your experience traveling.
a..The seats' present size vs. ideal size.
b. Train system vs. domestic air travel - preference.
c. Places you have visited – why so memorable.

What Happened Before the Meeting:

A. I hope you slept well last night. I heard that they are going to extend this meeting until almost 9:00 tonight. The boss wants to wrap up everything before he leaves. But you are young and energetic – no problem.

B. Are you kidding? I slept but not very well. Even though we have to agree on a lot of major issues, I am sure we can finish the meeting by 7:30 at the latest. If we finish early, I can change my flight and leave tonight. How about you?
A. I can't get out of here until tomorrow. Maybe tonight I will get some sleep. I guess I'll cut down on coffee today. Yesterday I had too much caffeine. Between jet lag and coffee I found it hard to concentrate. Long meetings are not my forte (strong point.)

B. The agenda is well prepared, so let's hope everything goes smoothly. If we get the shipping problem solved the rest will be easy. So let's go in and see what happens.

Analysis:

1. Ready for a long meeting. + why.
2. Not ready + why. May I go home early + how.
3. Will stay but jet lag, coffee, & long meetings – bad.
4. Reasons for expecting a short meeting.

Pattern Practice:

Extend v.– lengthen, make longer, 2. Stretch out.
The game is tied 2-2, so we will extend it. Extend your hand, I will help you.

Wrap up- finish, complete. We will wrap up this discussion now.

Jet lag – feeling tired/sleepy due to changing time zones too quickly. Coming from Los Angeles to Tokyo gives me jet lag. It takes me three days to get over jet lag. Many airline passengers suffer from jet lag.

Concentrate v. – to focus on, give something one's full attention,
Concentrate on you driving. You should concentrate on listening.

Forte – strong point, special talent. Keeping children happy is her forte. My forte is reading maps. Cooking is not my forte. Her forte is making people laugh.

Agenda – list of items to be discussed. Let's put safety on the agenda for the next meeting. There are 10 items on the agenda.

Cut down on – use less, eat/drink less. I must cut down on salt. She cut down on her smoking. (*Cut out – give up completely. Cut out sugar from your diet.)

Rest n. – remainder, what is left,
 I ate two apples; I gave the rest to my neighbors. This book is interesting; the rest of them are boring. This book is English, the rest are Japanese.

Solve v.- find the answer to. I was able to solve all the math problems. The government is trying to solve the housing problem.

HINT: *When visiting another country, pick up a newspaper. Read at least the headlines and the sports page. It will give you a few topics to talk about.

Challenge:

Talk about the last meeting you attended.
a. Different kinds of meetings & participants
b. How to avoid jet lag. (Time difference when traveling.)
c. A meeting – a problem –a solution (e.g. No electricity
 owing to an earthquake...discussing an item not on the
 agenda.)

Newspaper Headlines:

A. Wasn't it terrible what happened in Japan? Did you see the tsunami on TV? It was terrible. I never saw such destruction. I pity the victims.

B. No one expected an earthquake of that magnitude. And the tsunami came so quickly. Thousands were just swept away. I don't know how that area will recover.
A. People in many countries are donating money to help. The army and many volunteers are helping. But they will need help for a long time.

B. That is so sad, and so many children were lost, so many families uprooted. Now, they will have to build homes for the people left homeless. I hope there are no more big quakes. I heard there is now a problem with the nuclear power plant in Fukushima.

Analysis:
1. Headlines + emotion
2. Facts + emotion
3. Helping hands- volunteers, sad.
4. Children, homeless, + 1 more problem.

Pattern Practice:

Pity – feel sorry for. I pity the homeless people. I don't pity criminals.

Expect- think/hope something will happen. I expect a letter. She expects a big bonus this year. (My wife is expecting – pregnant- going to have a baby.)

Recover – get over, get better. My wife was sick but she recovered quickly.

Donate to give to charity. I donated $50 to the Salvation Army. He donated blood to help the earthquake victims.

Uprooted- pulled up, forced to move. War uproots many families. The hurricane uprooted many trees.

Lost – died, were killed 2. Misplace. Many fine people were lost in the war. That lady lost two sons in the fire. I lost my mother last year.

Challenge:

Your emotions when you saw the tsunami on TV.
a. Fukushima nuclear plant-facts+ feelings
b. Dangers of radiation.
c. Forced to leave…children...families

Newspaper Headlines II:

1. Did you see this article about China? – the one where 18 people passed by an injured child on the road. It's hard to believe.

2. I read about it in another newspaper. It appears people are cold hearted. But there is more to the story.

1. More? How come no one helped the child? She could have died. She was hit by a small truck.

2. Well, it seems that many Chinese like to sue those who help. So when victims   recover, they hire a lawyer, and accuse the kind helper of making them worse.

1. Is that true? That is hard to believe. Don't they appreciate being helped?

2. I am sure some do, but some people are always looking for ways to get money. It used to be that way in America too.

1. You're pulling my leg (joking)? That would never happen in America.

2. It happened many times. That is why many states passed 'The Good Samaritan Law'. I am sure you have heard of it?

1. No, I haven't. Does it have anything to do with the Good Samaritan in the Bible? I know that story.

2. That's where they got the name from. It just legislates that a helper in good faith cannot be sued by the victim. I think it is the law in most states.

1. It's a pity the Chinese don't have that law. It seems like they need it.

2. They are getting more like the U.S. They like to sue. Some people think U.S.A. means "U (you) Sue All".

Analysis:

Accident in China. Passers-by ignore the victim. Reasons why people did not get involved. Sue-happy people everywhere. Good Samaritan law explained.

Pattern Practice:

It is hard to believe. It is easy to believe.

Article n.- report, a column in a newspaper. I wrote an article about sushi.

It appears – it seems, it looks like. It appears everyone forgot my birthday.
 Accuse – to claim someone did wrong, charge with an offense/crime. My neighbor accused me of stealing his apples. The man was accused of murder. The accused (person) will be found guilty or innocent.

Appreciate- feel thankful for, have gratitude, I appreciate your help.
(Appreciate has a second meaning. It can mean: become more valuable or worth more. Gold, land, good art, and currencies can appreciate.)

Anything to do with – be related to in some way. Don't have anything to do with criminals. She doesn't have anything to do with shipping goods.

Pulling one's leg – joking, kidding. He didn't win the lottery, he is only pulling your leg. You played golf with the king? You're pulling my leg.*(Do not tell someone 'you are lying' when he/she is only joking.)

Legislate – to make a law. Congress legislates strict immigration laws.

In good faith without any intention of doing wrong, honest, sincere. The mistake was made in good faith. He signed the contract in good faith.

Challenge

Talk about an accident you saw or read about.
 a. How to help the homeless.
 b. When to sue or not to sue.
 c. Examples of helpers becoming victims.

NOTES:

Newspaper Headlines III:

A. It's strange what makes news nowadays. I just read where parents at a kids' soccer game attacked the referee and each other.

B. Soon that may not be news. It happens quite often. I am not surprised.

A. I thought the aim of youth sports was to teach a sport and sportsmanship. Those parents should be ashamed of themselves. It's a disgrace.

B. Some parents push their kids too hard to be winners. The children are not learning much, and often they give up sports altogether. It's a pity.

A. That's one extreme. The other extreme is when parents don't even want to keep score in a sport. At the end of the season everyone gets a trophy. That's equally insane.

B. That certainly doesn't prepare youth for the real world, but it lessens the pressure they have to win all the time. There must be a happy medium.

A. Parents should praise effort and realize you don't always win every game. They and the players all need to hear that from the coach.

B. Sometimes parents want to live out their dreams through their children. All it does is stress their children. Sports should be fun for young people.

A. Easier said than done. If the parents want to attack each other, they should take up boxing!

Analysis:
One person is surprised that violence breaks out at youth sports' events. Two kinds of parents – two extremes. The conversation mentions the happy medium, the ideal for young athletes, as well as parents' and coaches' responsibility.

Pattern Practice:

Ashamed – feel embarrassed, feel guilty, humiliated,
I felt ashamed when I was caught stealing money from the collection basket at church. I was ashamed when I was arrested. He felt ashamed when he fell asleep at the party.

Extreme – highest, furthest from the center, far from moderate, The death penalty for stealing is extreme. The poles are extremely cold. Fasting and over-eating are extremes.

Happy medium- Comes from the old definition of virtue being in the middle of two extremes. Food and study are good things, but you have to pick a happy medium. (Eating too much or studying too long is not good for one's health.)

Insane – not sane, not normal, crazy, mentally ill, foolish,
It's insane to climb Mt Fuji only wearing a T-shirt. Working 18 hours a day is insane. She has an insane desire to be photographed with politicians.

Lessen –make smaller, reduce. Medicine will lessen the pain.
All it does – only, the only thing. This medicine is no good; all it does is make me dizzy. Don't hit the beehive; all is does is make the bees more aggressive.

Challenge:

To talk about sports fans in different countries.
a. Parents putting their daughters in pre-teen beauty contests.
b. Role models for children.
c. Do teens spend too much on cosmetics?

Useful Hints:

 Context: Another important hint is to try to guess the meaning of a word-especially if you know all the words around it. For example: "I **missed** the bus by one minute. I am sorry I am late." If **missed** is the only word you do not know, you can guess it means you did not get on the bus. E.g. "Drunk drivers **cause** many accidents." If **cause** is the only word you do not know, you may guess it means they are the reason for the accidents, or drunk drivers are in many accidents. If you come across a sentence such as:"In summer I **imbibe** water," imbibe is probably the only word you do not understand. From knowing all the other words you may guess that 'imbibe' means 'drink' or 'need'. Either way, the meaning of the sentence is clear. ('Imbibe" means drink.) Most times you will guess correctly.

Another hint for understanding meaning is to be aware of **body language** and facial expressions. The movement of the hands and the eyes can give a lot of information. You can practice reading body language by watching movies or video tapes.

A final hint is to **admit not knowing.** A true story will help to emphasize this point. A friend of mine hosted a foreign student. She told him to turn off the air conditioner before going to bed. He nodded and replied "yes". The next morning he woke up with a terrible cold. He had no idea what the lady said, and he had left the air conditioner on all night. So pretending to understand is not a good course of action.

Good Morning Scene:

1. John, it's time to get up. Come on, wake up. It's almost 7:00 o'clock. Your alarm did not go off. You'll be late for school.

 2. OK Mom. I'm getting up. Don't worry. I have plenty of time. School doesn't begin until 8:15. I won't be late.

1. Come on John, what's keeping you? Your breakfast is getting cold. If you don't hurry up you will miss the bus. I won't call you again. You should be ready by now.

2. I'm almost ready. I'm just putting on my shirt. I'll be down in a minute. Mom, did you see my jacket? I can't find it. Did Bill borrow it again?

1. Your jacket is here in the kitchen – where you left it. Come and get it. It's now 7:15. You don't have that much time.

2. What's for breakfast? I hope it's not fried eggs again. I'm tired of eating eggs. (I'm fed up eating eggs.) How about making pancakes for a change?

1. I'm not running a restaurant. If you don't like the menu – cook your own breakfast. Don't you have basketball practice today? You need a good breakfast. It's the most important meal of the day.

2. Don't worry about me Mom. I always eat plenty. Tomorrow is Saturday. I'll cook breakfast for everyone. I'll make blueberry pancakes, they're everyone's favorite.

1. How about another cup of tea? More toast? You're losing your appetite. You used to eat more last year. By the way, make sure you have your own key. I may be out when you come home. Don't forget your lunch, it's on the table.

2. Mom, I hate to ask you, but could you drive me to school? I don't want to be late for my first class. I know I should get up earlier. But today was an exception. Come on Mom, just this once. You know I love you.

1. OK John. Just this once. But don't count on it every day. Before we go, make sure the back door is locked. But tomorrow, guess who is washing my car! OK? Then it's a deal.

Analysis:

This conversation starts with reasons for getting up, followed by reasons and comments why rushing is not needed. Next we have Mom repeating why speed is necessary. A missing jacket is a reason for the delay. Breakfast menu dialogue/complaining. Mother's concern about health and son's answer. Son's promise to cook breakfast on Saturday.

The son gets his Mom to drive him to school as he promises to wash the car the following day. Note that in most conversations we use more words than necessary, even though we are expressing only one idea!

Pattern Practice:

It's time to plant the rice. It's time to go to bed. It's time to paint the house.
It's time to put away winter clothes. It's time to go home.
*Note two times.
(One time is time on the clock; the other time means season or fitting period.)

Almost –a little before, not quite, very nearly,

It is almost 10:00 o'clock. I almost broke the window. He is almost 200 pounds. She almost got married. (*The verb is in the past tense even though the action never happened. When almost is used with the verb 'to be', almost means 'very nearly'. The verb 'to be' can be present or past. E.g. I was almost late.)

Plenty of – more than enough, a lot of, followed by a count or non- count noun.
We have plenty of rice. She has plenty of books. Give him plenty of space. There is plenty of snow. They got plenty of sleep last night. I have plenty of pens.

Not … until: - double negative that stresses (emphasizes) the word after until.
I did not get up until 9:00 AM. - I got up at 9:00 A.M. We did not finish until midnight. They did not score until the last minute. I can't go until Bill comes. I did not meet her until yesterday.

Keeping – preventing, delaying, preventing one from coming.
The traffic is keeping him. What kept you? Sickness kept him from work today. What is keeping the mailman? He is usually here by now.

In – within, less than, (In 10 minutes means in 9:59 or less.)
I'll be ready in a minute. I came to school in 20 minutes. He
finished the work in a day. We can make it to Tokyo by car
in 30 minutes.

Tired of – fed up, dislike, find something disagreeable,
I am tired of waiting for John. He is tired of practicing the
piano. The children are tired of playing hide-'n-seek. I'm
tired of eating fast food.

How about …ing: -invitation, request, advice,
How about pitching for us? How about buying comics for the
kids? How about eating out tonight? How about taking
medicine for your pain?

For a change: - something different, for fun, a change of
pace. Let's eat out for a change. We always go skating; let's
go bowling for a change.

Used to v. ..- did once but do not do now. He used to live in
this town. My Dad used to be a policeman. John and I used to
go to high school together. They used to have a dog. I used to
smoke.

By the way – to change the topic of conversation, to bring in
a new topic abruptly. "I think Japan will win the soccer
game. By the way, when did you get here?"

Make sure: to check to be certain,
Make sure you have your keys. Make sure you take an
umbrella. Make sure your alarm is on. Make sure you have
your passport. Make sure the windows are closed. Make sure
you write to grandma. Make sure the door is locked.

Count on- depend on, rely on, trust,
You can count on your Mom never to forget birthdays. I count on my sister to help me with homework. You can count on the government to raise taxes. That team counts on their pitchers to win many games. You can't count on their batters (hitting.)

It's a deal- We have an agreement. It's a promise. "You bring the beer; I will bring the steaks." "OK. It's a deal."

Challenge:
 Talk about your experiences of getting
 up.
 a. Getting ready to go out… waiting... hurrying.
 b. Going by bus…train…or by taxi.
 c. Going to a birthday party… buying a present.

Driving to School:

1. Let's use Lincoln Avenue. It's longer than Main Street, but it's much faster. Main Street has too many traffic jams. Besides, now it is rush hour. Plenty of stop and go driving.

2. I think you're right. Today is Friday. It is usually very crowded. But I know a short cut through Elm Street. We can make it in 10 minutes. I love this street; it is never crowded.

1. Take it easy Mom. You just passed a patrol car. I think he is coming after us. Slow down. He has his lights flashing. Now Mom we'll need all your charm.

2A . Morning ma'am. May I see your driver's license? Thank you. Do you know the speed limit on this street? Well, it's 25 miles per hour. You were going almost 35.

2. I am very sorry officer. I usually take Main St. I know it's 35 mph there. I did not realize Elm St. was slower. I am just taking my son to school. In future I'll be more careful.

2A. I should write you a ticket, but instead I'll give you a warning. The next time I won't let you off. Please drive carefully. There are many children going to school now. Have a safe day.

2. Thank you officer. It won't happen again. I will be more careful and observant. ….

1. Wow! that was close. I was sure he was going to give us a ticket. If I was driving it would be a different story. I guess you look responsible. But Mom, you do have a heavy foot. You drive faster than Dad.

2. Well, thank God that is over. Now you are late for school. You can explain it to the principal. She'll give you a tardy slip. In future, set your alarm and go by bus. That was a good lesson for both of us.

1. Here Mom, I won't need my keys. I have practice after school until 5:30. I can get a ride home with Jim. I see his car in the parking lot. Thanks Mom for the ride. I've got to run.

Analysis:
Reasons for using one street over another. Mom decides to take a shortcut and to speed. Son and patrol car notice Mom's speed. Police officer lectures Mom and lets her off with a warning. Comments from son and mother. How son will get home after basketball practice.

Pattern Review:
Traffic jam – many cars hardly moving on a road or street. In Japan during Golden Week there are many traffic jams everywhere.

Make it:- go, come, succeed, attend, 2. Choose, decide, 3. Construct, build, 4.cause, make happen,
I can make it home from school in 10 minutes. (go/come) He took a penalty kick but he did not make it.(score) I can't make your birthday party.(attend) He tried to get into Todai (Tokyo University) but he did not make it.(succeed)

She never made any of the afternoon classes. (attended). Let's make the meeting time 5:00 PM. (set). Make my order curry rice. (Chose/select) Taxes make me angry. (cause emotion/feeling). Let's make the meeting at 10:00 AM on Tuesday. (Decide on.) For lunch, I think I'll make it sandwiches. (Choose.) Which kind? Let's make it egg sandwiches. (Choice)
The makes tables. My Mom made a cake. (Put together, create. She makes me laugh. Taxes make me angry. He makes trouble. Snacks make me fat.
The heat makes me sweat. (Causes--the reason why something happens) You always make excuses. She makes a lot of progress. * (At the end of the book, there are many more examples of sentences using 'make'.)

Different story- something very different. The window you broke belongs to the chief of police. That's a different story.

Over – finished, ended. Class is over at 10:15 AM. School is over at 4:00 PM.

Realize: - be aware of, notice, be conscious of, think about,
I just realized that this clock is slow. He did not realize his
dog was missing. They just realized that there is no school
today. I did not realize there is a hole in this bag. He realized
it was rude to stick his chopsticks in the rice.

Heavy foot- fast driver (also- lead foot),
That driver has a heavy foot. (He presses down hard on the
accelerator – he speeds.)

In future – from now on,
In future we will take Main St. In future, charge your phone
before school. In future I will drive more carefully. In future I
will bring my computer.

Lesson – learning experience. Falling out of the tree was a
good lesson for me. Not studying and getting an F on the test
was a good lesson for the pupil.

Instead of- in place of, as a substitute for,
My Mom uses honey instead of sugar.-She doesn't use sugar;
she uses honey instead. My Dad cooked supper instead of
ordering pizza. Use a pen instead of a pencil. Let's meet on
Tuesday instead of Monday. You pitch instead of me.

I've got to run: - 'got' has no specific meaning in the
sentence, it is often used after 'have'.(Using 'got' after 'have'
or 'has' makes your English sound more fluent!)

I 've got a cold – I have a cold. She's got to leave school
early today. We've got to fix that broken gate. We've got a
problem we cannot solve.

Challenge:

Getting/not getting a traffic ticket for driving too fast.
 a. The fastest way to go from A to B…
 b. The best time to visit Disneyland ...London…Hokkaido
 c. Should I buy a motorbike or a car…

The Telling & Retelling:

1. Hey Bill. Guess what happened this morning? We almost got a ticket coming to school. I was sweating. I was sure we were finished. But the police officer let Mom off with a warning.

2. You mean to say you were not driving? How come? I thought you were the official driver for your family? Where did this happen?

1. It was on Elm St. The patrol car was hiding in a driveway. It is so hard to spot it with all those trees. Lucky for us he was in a good mood.

2. Your Mom likes to speed. Were you going much over the speed limit?

1. No, just nine miles. I guess if it goes into double digits, they write you up. Elm St. is tricky. It is so wide with no lights. It is easy to speed there.

2. You should take the bus, then that would not happen. You slept in again this morning? What else is new!

1. Just a few minutes. In future I'll get up early. I really mean it this time.

2. Oh, yeah, that will be the day. You sleep so much you could teach bears how to sleep. Get a stronger alarm clock - one that throws you out of bed!

1. There's the bell for class. See you later. Bye.

Pattern Review:

"Write you up."- Write out a ticket. (A fine to be paid for speeding.)

"What else is new? −This is not news. A politician accused of lying. "What else is new?" -   It happens all the time.

"Hard to spot" – Hard to see or notice.

"I thought we were finished."- I thought it would be a bigger problem. I thought we would get a traffic ticket. I expected an unpleasant result.

"That will be the day!"- I don't expect that action to happen. If someone says:"The government will probably reduce (lessen) taxes next year." The usual response or comment is: "That will be the day." (That would be great if it ever happened, but it is not likely.)

Challenge:
a. Choosing a good high school …criteria…discipline…
b. Choosing a major/minor in college…why…
c. Choosing an ideal place to live…cost…weather…safety…

Shopping:

1. I am out of sugar. It is all gone. (There is none left.) Why don't I run to the store. I need a few other things as well. Why don't you come with me? You must get some new shoes. Those are worn out. You can't wear them anymore. Let's go to the mall. They are having a big sale this weekend. If you go with me I will treat you to ice cream. Of course you can help carry the groceries.

2. That sounds like a good idea. I can drive you. My car is parked outside. I want to go to that new shoe store. You know the one I mean. It is right next to the Food Court Plaza. I can't think of the name of it now. My friends recommended it.

1. OK. There's a parking space over there. It is not so near the entrance but we need exercise. Let's pick up your shoes first. The supermarket is the other side of the mall. I don't like to leave food in the car during this hot weather. It spoils.

2. Here we are. The shoe section is here. Why don't you try on these? What size do you take now? (What size fits you?) Size 6 ½ or 7 fits me. What do you think of these? They look stylish.

1. They won't go with a lot of your clothes. How about a lighter shade of brown? Let's ask the salesman to help us out.

2. Could you bring me this style in a lighter shade? Let me try on size 6 ½ and 7 please.

2A. Certainly. Please try these on. Here is a shoe horn.

2. I find that they pinch my toes. I need a wider pair. How about 7EEE? They should fit me. Yes, these are a perfect fit. Is there any way I can get a bigger discount?

2A. As a matter of fact there is. If you sign up for a store credit card we can take off an extra 12%.

1. That probably takes a long time to fill out paperwork.

2A. Not all at. We just make a copy of your driver's license and you just sign it. It's very simple and it takes no time at all.

1. OK. Here's my license. This pair costs $70.00. With 12% off, what is the retail price? My math is a little rusty. (weak)

2A. You pay only $61.60. Will this be cash or credit? No, I don't need ID. I just copied your license! Thank you for shopping at Brogues Shoes.

Analysis:

Reasons for going shopping. Why her daughter went. An example of a conditional promise …if. What happened at the store. Why she changed the color/shade. How she got a bigger discount.

Pattern Practice:

We are out of rice…out of salt…out of time…The printer is out of paper and also out of ink. My son is always out of money! The book you want is out of print. (No longer being published/printed.) The car is almost out of gas. (It is almost empty.) That store is out of batteries. (Out of = sold out.)

Why don't I v. – I will v. Let me v.
Why don't I call you later. Why don't I help you.

Why don't you v. – advice, request, you should, (Why don't we =let's),
Why don't you go home by taxi? Why don't you buy a magazine? Why don't you take a nap? Why don't you take some medicine? Why don't we go bowling? Why don't we take turns driving? Why don't you read this book?

Go with – looks good together. Black goes with white. Yellow goes with green or blue. Purple and red don't go well together. Shoes don't go with a kimono. A string tie does not go with a tuxedo. Wine goes with pasta.

Challenge:
Where to take a sick friend…hospital…clinic…
a..To buy a used item from a recycle shop or a new one at a bazaar or store.
 b. Which restaurant to choose for a family meal…
 c. Buying a new phone…

Retelling Shopping:

1. I heard you and Mom went shopping. How was it? Did you buy a lot of clothes?

2. No, Dad. This time I bought only shoes. We went to that new store near the Food Court. The shoes were on sale and besides, we got 12% off.

1. How did you manage that? Do you know the salesperson? You must have made the shoes look good!

2. No, we just signed up for a store credit card. But relax, we don't have to use it. But if you need shoes, you might like to use it.

1. If I ever go shopping I'll keep that in mind. Did you patronize the Food Court too?

2. Dad! Of course not. They serve only fast food there- salt and fat. You know I am on a diet. I want to look good in my new swim suit.

1. By the way, what color shoes did you get? May I see them?

2. I was going to get a dark brown pair, but Mom convinced me to buy these. They are a lighter shade of brown. They will go better with most of my clothes. Oh! Look at the time. I'll be late for my tennis lesson. Bye.

Analysis:

A daughter tells her father about her shopping experience, the new credit card, and her new shoes. She adds reasons why she does not eat fast food.

Pattern Practice:

I was going to buy black shoes but I changed my mind. We were going to order steak but we got fish instead. He was going to phone you but he lost your number. They were going to play baseball but it started to rain heavily.
(Was/were going to v.- means that the action never happened.)

Usually a salesperson says: "They look good on you." "You make them look good" is a humorous way of praising the customer.

How did you manage that? –a question about how you were able to do something difficult. You got tickets for the final? How did you manage that? You flew first class? How did you manage that? You got Lionel Messi's autograph? How did you manage that?

Did you ever patronize that new restaurant? To be a customer. (Ever – means one time.) Did you ever climb Mt. Fuji? No, I never climbed it. (Never- usually means not even one time.)

Mom convinced me to buy this. She persuaded me to buy it. She changed my mind. I convinced my friend to buy a bicycle instead of a motorbike.

On a diet. They went on a picnic. They went on a trip. They went on a tour. The workers are on strike. They went on vacation. I went on a journey. She went on a shopping spree. The young couple went on their honeymoon.

Challenge:

To talk about sports fans in different countries
a. Parents putting their daughters in pre-teen beauty contests.
 b. Role models for children.
 a. Do teens spend too much on music?

NOTES:

IF & WHEN:

To expand a topic **'if'** is very useful. It brings up a condition, a possible/probable result, a request/invitation, or an imperative (order).
Note: 'if' means that something may or may not happen; 'when' usually means the time something happens, or something that usually happens often.
E.g. If we win I will be happy. (We may lose.) When I go home I always eat a snack. (I will definitely go home.) If it rains I will go home by taxi. (It may rain.) When it rains I always take my umbrella. (Every time it rains.)

If you go with me   I will treat you to coffee
                      I am going to treat you to lunch.
                      I may buy cake for dessert.
                      I should let you drive.
                      let's look for bargains.
If you go shopping   try on some clothes.
                      you can buy new shoes.
                      I want to go with you.
                      take the shopping list with you.
                      I am going to play golf.
                      I hope you pick up a newspaper.
                      don't forget to fill up the gas tank.
                      make sure you use the coupons.
                      don't be afraid to buy new snacks.
                      I want you to buy brown rice.
If you go shopping   it's best to go to the mall.
                      try to come home by 5:00 PM.
If she goes shopping she likes to buy shoes.
                      she should buy bread.
                      she ought to buy rice.
If he goes shopping he is willing to buy wine for you.
                      he intends to go by motorbike.

he can cook dinner later.
he hopes to finish by 4:00
he may buy pizza for dinner.
he will buy lots of cereal
he has to make a list first.
he must pay by credit card.
he doesn't have to take cash.
he is going to buy fish.
he will consider coming
 home by taxi .
 his wife will go to a spa.
 get him to buy snacks.
When he goes shopping   he like to buy unusual food.
  he likes to save money.
  he goes by car.
  he hates to wait in line.
  he likes to talk to others.
  he takes lot of small coins.
  he will spend too much.
  I should go with him.
  he finds bargains.
  he buys enough for a month
he may buy things he doesn't need.
he spends less than his wife.
he depends on his son to
remember everything.
he tries to park near the entrance.
he always thanks the cashiers.
he uses his phone to send us photos
of items he likes.
he complains about prices.
he enjoys noticing other shoppers
he tries to save money by buying
generic brands.

he finds it hard to find things in the
store.
he may drop into the bar (pub) for
 a drink.
he buys the most expensive brands.
he always forgets at least on item.

Many similar patterns can be based on the above. For
example:
If I go skiing…When I go swimming… If she goes to
university… When she goes on vacation… If he gets a pet…
When she graduates from university... If she lives with her
parents… If they move to Tokyo… If we join a gym… When
we get home… If we are late… If it starts to rain… When she
gets married… When you visit Boston… If you get lost… If
the weather is fine…   If the car breaks down… If it starts
snowing… If I have time… When I pay my taxes … When
my mother visits…   When there is an earthquake… (The
possibilities for using these patterns are many—use
imagination!)

NOTES:

Shopping II:

1. We're out of tea. When you use the last tea bag you should tell me. There is a shopping list on the refrigerator. Just jot (write) it down on the list, then we won't run out. I hate to go shopping just for one item.

2. I'm sorry I was rushing to work after breakfast. I forgot to mention it. But don't worry. We have plenty of coffee and green tea. Sometimes I like a cup of coffee for a change.

1. That's O.K. for you, but the rest of the family never drink coffee. In future I will buy extra tea. If my friends drop in, I will have no tea to serve them. I hope they like green tea.

2. I'm going to the convenience store to get a newspaper. I can pick up some tea for you. Which brand do you like?

1. Any kind is fine with me. It's up to you. Don't just buy the cheapest brand. There is nothing worse than bad tea.

2. I have a better idea. Why don't you go to the store and I'll do the dishes. Then I won't have to worry about getting the wrong kind. Or if you are tired, I'll drive you there. I'll wait in the car as they have not much parking space.

1. I appreciate the offer but it can wait until tomorrow. I have a few other things to pick up as well. So let's put off shopping until then. But thanks all the same. It was kind of you to offer.

Analysis:
Communication needed to make a better shopping list. In this family tea is preferred to coffee. The offer to pick up tea or drive to the convenience store is appreciated but politely refused.

Pattern Practice:

Jot – write down quickly. Let me jot down your new phone number. Let me jot down the price of this dress. Jot down the number of the car in our parking place.

Any one is fine with me. Any one is OK (acceptable). When will we go? Any time is fine with me. Where will we go? Any place is fine with me. Which color do you want? Any color is fine with me.

Offer – ready to do, ready to pay, ready to give. He offered to wash the car… She offered to pay for my lunch… She offered to buy my used car for $5,000.00

Challenge: Offer to do something nice for your family.
   a. Drop off/pick up some clothes at the cleaners.
   b. Interview an applicant for a part time job.
   c. Should we try the new cleaners that just opened?

A Chance Meeting/Encounter:

1. Hi Bill. Great to run into you here. I haven't seen you in ages. How have you been?

2. Oh, I'm fine, still working away at the same old job. How about you? Are you still with Acme?

1. No, I left Acme a few weeks ago and luckily I found a new job with a computer software company. This is actually my first week there. Yesterday was my first day in the job. Everything is so new. But the company is only 20 minutes from my home. So commuting is a breeze. I am in charge of new software for hospitals or doctors' computers.

2. That sounds interesting. Do you go around selling or do they order from you? Do you have to travel a lot?

1. They order from us directly. I send out flash drives with a portion of the program on it. Then each hospital staff person looks at it. If they need help, or if they like it, I visit and give a demonstration.

2. Sounds like you really hit the jackpot. But it's right up your alley. You know everything about computers. I'm happy for you.

1. I am lucky but I am still learning. I don't want to make any mistakes. The company is small but it is growing.

2. This calls for a celebration. Let's go out on Friday night. I know a great place near the station. Bring the wife and I'll bring Jane. I know she has nothing else planned. It will be fun.

1. Let me check with Becky first. But I am sure Friday will be OK. I'll get back to on that.

Analysis:

Two old friends (acquaintances) meet by accident and talk about one man's new job. They plan to invite their wives to join in celebrating the new job by eating out the following Friday night.

Pattern Review:

Commuting is a breeze- very easy. That last test was a breeze- it was a piece of cake. (The same meaning.) The job interview was a breeze.

Sounds like – I think so when I hear what you said. "Let's climb Mt. Fuji after Christmas."- That sounds dangerous. After hearing about a friend's vacation- "Sounds like you had fun." Also for music or people coming in- That sounds like Mozart. That sounds like my wife's car.

Hit the jackpot – to be very lucky or successful. To win a prize.
"You got two tickets for the final game?" Wow! You really hit the jackpot!

Right up your alley:-something that suits you.
"He is a Little League coach." "That's right up his alley. He used to play baseball for the Boston Red Sox."

This calls for a celebration- we should do something special to show our happiness. This calls for an investigation.- We should check it out.

In ages – for a long time. I have not gone bowling in ages. (Slight exaggeration.) I have not eaten ice cream in ages!

Crazy about – like best, love. Jack is crazy about skiing.

Touch base with – contact, discuss with, speak to.
Touch base with the boss before you order another shipment.

I'll get back to you. – I'll contact you again. I will phone you later.

Challenge:

Describe your present or past job…
a. How you met someone famous…
b. Is a judge's punishment too light/heavy…
c. How to plan a surprise birthday party for…

A Chance Encounter -Retelling

1. I just ran into Jack. He told me about his new job. He is working for a computer software company.

2. He was working for a restaurant chain. (He used to work for a restaurant chain.) When did he get this new job?

1.Yesterday was his first day on the job. He did not tell me much about it. We are going to go out on Friday to celebrate. You are free on Friday, aren't you?

2. Of course. I haven't seen Beth in ages. I am looking forward to this. It will be fun. Where are we going to go?

1. That new restaurant near the station looks good. Jack and Beth both are crazy about Japanese food. It will be perfect. Touch base with Beth and make a reservation. You know it is usually crowded on a Friday night.

How to Reserve (book) a Room in a Hotel:

A. Grand Hotel. How may I help you?

B. I'd like to book a room for two nights, Saturday, March 17th and Sunday,   March 18th.

A. Certainly. Would you like a single room, a double room or a suite?

B. I'd like a double room. How much is it?

A.A double room is $200.00 per night, excluding taxes.

B. OK. I'll take it.

A. Let me have your name.

B. My name is MacRyan, Jack MacRyan.

A. Macran? How do you spell it?

B. M as in Mary, A as in Andy, C as in Charlie, R as in Robert, Y as in young (Yosemite), A as in Andy, N as in Nancy.

A. OK . I've got it. Jack MacRyan. Which credit card will you be using?

B. Visa. The number is: 1111-2222-3333-4444.It expires 05/25.

A. Thank you. May I have the 3-digit code on the back of the card?

B. It's 1-2-3. Is that all?

A. Let me have your email address and your phone number just in case we need to contact you.

 B. My phone number is 42-123-4567. My email address is: macrya@email.com. All lowercase. (No capital letters.)

A. Thank you. Just a reminder, check-in is after 3:00 PM, and check-out is before 10:00 AM. We do not allow pets. Do you have any other questions?

B. As a matter of fact (actually) I do. Do you have any discounts available? Also, how much is the room including taxes?

A. The total for two nights is $480.00 including taxes. We do have discounts during mid-week. If you changed your stay to March 13th, 14th , and 15th , we could offer you a 10% discount.

B. No, I can't do that. By the way, to whom am I speaking? (Who am I talking to?) And do I get a confirmation number?

A. I'm Kemiko Smith. We don't use confirmation numbers, but I will send you a confirmation email. Is there anything else?

B. Yes, before I forget, I'd like a non-smoking room on the 2nd or 3rd floor- preferably one with a good view. (...one facing the ocean …facing south.)

A. Certainly. I will make sure you have a non-smoking room on the 2nd or 3rd floor. Thank you for calling the Grand Hotel. We look forward to making sure you have an enjoyable stay. Goodbye, and thank you for calling the Grand Hotel.

Analysis:

A man books a room for two nights. They make sure his name and credit card number are correct. He remembers to ask for a discount and the name of the person to whom he is speaking. Also, he finds out the total cost with tax. He also expresses his room preference.

Pattern Practice:

Lct me have your name. = May I have you name? = What is your name?

It cost $10.00 excluding tax. It cost $11.00 including 10% sales tax.

Excluding = without;   including = with, plus.

How do you spell your name? Use names of persons with common names or names of well-known cities or countries, or objects easily spelled. E.G. "Peters"- P as in Patrick ; E as in Edward; T as in Tom; E as in Edward; R as in Robert, and S as in Sam. **(OR**: P as in Poland, E as in England, T as in Tanzania, E as in England, R as in Russia, and S as in Spain.) You can also use the names of famous cities. "Peters" – P as in Panama, E as in Edinburgh, T as in Toronto, E as in Edinburgh, R as in Rome, and S as in Sydney.)

Offer – ready to give, ready to do, ready to pay. My friend offered me a cup of coffee. He offered to drive me to the station but I wanted to walk. She offered me $5,000.00 for my used car. (I accepted/refused her offer.)

Confirmation (confirm) – to make stronger, assure. The boss sent me a letter to confirm my promotion. The company confirmed they had received my order.

As a matter of fact – truly, not just an opinion, in reality, really.
As a matter of fact, Mr. Honda did start Honda Car Company.

Preferably -   if possible, ideally. I'd like a bigger car, preferably a black one. I want a seat in the back of the plane, preferably an aisle seat.

I look forward to … I am happy thinking about it.. . Eagerly awaiting.. . I am looking forward to going on vacation. She is looking forward to visiting Kyoto.

Challenge:

Reserve a table for two at a restaurant
a. Book a car rental for a week.
b. Book a flight on a domestic airline.
c. Reserve a tee time at a golf course.

NOTES:

Family Topic:

1.Can you tell a little about your family? Are they living in Japan now?

2.No, of course not. They live near Los Angeles. It is a very small city. But it is famous. It's the home town of Michelle Kwan – the skater.

1. I have heard of her. I saw her skate once in Tokyo. I am sure she won the NHK Cup. Did you ever meet her? Or maybe you went to the same high school?
2. No such luck. Our town has four high schools. My high school was famous for soccer players and nerds. You can guess which one I was!

1. I am sorry, but I do not understand the word "nerd". Is that how you pronounce it? What does it mean? I never heard it before.

2. Nerd just means a clever student who gets all 'A's, and is good at computers. They are always studying. They call us (the soccer players) 'jocks' because we are into sports. But I liked the nerds. They always helped me with my homework.

Analysis:

The conversation begins with family but gets sidetracked. They end up talking about Michelle Kwan and two kinds of high school students.
Notice how the conversation never continued about family. This is natural. Conversation flows like a river. It is not a railroad.

Pattern Practice:

No such luck – that did not happen. I was not lucky. Did you catch any homerun balls at the baseball game? No such luck.

Challenge:

Discuss Japanese food and western food
a. Life span of Japanese and Americans (English or Australians)
b. Percentage of fat people in Japan and the U.S.
c. What food do you associate with different countries?

Family Again:

1. So your family live in Torrance? Do you get to see them often?

2. No, I try to make it once a year around Thanksgiving. The whole family gets together for a few days. People are off work from Thursday to Sunday.

1. When is Thanksgiving? Is it the same as the Japanese Thanksgiving for Work? But we only get one day off.

2. It's the 4th Thursday in November. Usually it's about a month before Christmas. It's very big in the U.S. Most people celebrate it.

1. I don't understand. What do they celebrate? Work or family?

2. For Americans, Thanksgiving is a harvest festival. It began about 400 years ago when the first settlers came to the country. Now, I think people are just thankful for freedom, for their family, and for having enough food.
When is the Japanese Feast of Thanksgiving? I can't remember celebrating it. Is it very special here?

1. No, it's just one day in November. It is usually on November 23rd. I think is it more like Labor Day in the U.S. People are happy to get a day off work. We don't do anything special.

Analysis:

The conversation begins with family but veers off into discussing U.S. and Japanese Thanksgiving. *Note : we did not get around to the family yet. Conversation is not a straight jacket!

Pattern Practice:

Make it – go/come, attend. I cannot make your birthday party. I can make it here from my home in 20 minutes.

It's very big in Japan – It is very popular with everyone. New Year's is very big in Japan. Soccer is big in Japan.

Challenge:

Discuss changing national holidays .
a. Changing jobs in the U.S. and in Japan.
b. School year in Japan and in other countries.
c. Japanese work longer and harder than Americans. T/F?

Family Once Again:

1. You were telling me about your family. Do they live in Tokyo too?

2. No, my parents live in Chiba. My grandfather settled there after the war. So I am actually a farmer's son – the second son.

1. Oh, I see. Did your older brother get the farm, or did he leave too?

2. Of course. Isn't that the way it is in your country? The oldest inherits; the youngest gets a one-way ticket.

1. It often happens like that. But you can't complain. You got a great education. You went to one of the best schools in Japan.

2. I am not complaining, but I love farming. I hope to retire to a small farm. But this constant overtime and traveling in crowded trains may kill me first!

Analysis:

We get some information about the Japanese participant. We hear about the second sons of farmers. This second son reveals his love for farming.

*This time we got a little more information on one family. The conversation could continue talking about overtime, traveling to work, or any other related topic. Conversation flows and the topic naturally changes.

Challenge:

Expectations of men and women in society.
a. Challenges of students in different countries.
b. Care of the elderly in different societies.
c. Nuclear families, extended families, blended families.

Statistics:
1. What are you reading? Good news I hope.

2. According to this article, U.S. teenagers drink more than 20 cans of soda a week. Can you believe it?

1. That is incredible. I never would have guessed. That's far too much soda. They should drink less. It is bad for their health.

2. No wonder diabetes and obesity are now teenage problems. Parents are losing control and spoiling their kids. When I was a teenager I was lucky if I could afford one can of soda a week. Where do these teens get the money?

1. In some cases they work part time, but most of them get quite a lot of pocket money from their parents and grandparents. They have six pockets.

2. Doesn't the school teach them about health and diet? What are we paying taxes for? This is a disgrace. I think I'll write a letter to the newspaper (editor) and let people know how I feel about this.

1. I don't think it will do much good. The newspaper depends on beverage companies to buy ads in their paper. Besides, those same teens watch over 30 hours of TV every week. So how many hundred commercials do they view? It's called subliminal brainwashing.

2. Subliminal? What does that mean? Don't forget English is my second language!

1. Sorry for using such a difficult word, but it fits here. Subliminal means that the ads or commercials sink into our minds or brains without any effort on our part. Just think about, when you buy something, you usually buy an item you saw or heard advertised on TV.

2. I see. Now I understand why the companies pay so much to advertise during the Super Bowl. I guess it pays to show us commercials. We are being brainwashed.

A newspaper reader and a friend discuss how much soda U.S. teens drink. (Teen beverage consumption.) Writing a letter to the editor complaining about this would seem futile (useless). Reasons for drinking so much are mentioned; namely, they can afford it, and they are brainwashed by TV commercials.

Pattern Practice:

Incredible- hard to believe, unusual,
The baseball player drove in 12 runs with three homers. – "That's incredible."
The child ate ten hot dogs. "That's incredible."

No wonder- that is an explanation of why I am not surprised.
No wonder she is tired; she works over 60 hours a week.

Obesity – being excessively overweight, (obese –adjective)
Over 25% of Americans are obese. Obesity can cause health problems.

Subliminal – enters the subconscious mind. Parental praise or criticism subliminally affects children.

Brainwash – to change a hearer's perception, especially through repetition. In totalitarian countries, dictators try to brainwash young people.

Six pockets – four grandparents + two parents.

Challenge:

Teens should have to volunteer before graduating from HS.
a. Letters to a newspaper are useful/ useless.
b. How to balance education, freedom, and common sense.
c. Why fewer people are reading newspapers now.

Problem at Home:

1. Hi Mary. You look like an onion (bamboo shoot). How many layers of clothes do you have on?

2. Just five. The heating system in my apartment is broken. I am freezing.

2A. You should go to the Senior Center. At least the heat is working there. If you don't go, you may catch cold.

3. I have a better idea. Why don't you buy a small heater? I can lend you a humidifier. They work well together. Then the air won't get too dry.

4. Wait a minute. I know a good repairman. Let me give you his phone number. I am sure he will fix it for you.

2. That's the problem. My heater is old. I am not sure it is worth fixing. I did call a repairman but he can't come until the 31st. That's two weeks from now.

5. How about trying the Recycle Shop? They often have small stoves at reasonable prices. I am going to drive past it on my way home. I'll drop in and see if they have anything suitable.

3. I don't think you should buy a used stove. You may be buying someone else's junk, or someone else's problem! If you can afford it, buy a new one.

4. I just remembered. My brother just bought a new stove. I can ask him to loan or give you the old one. That will save you money and keep you warm. I think it still works.

2. Thanks for all the suggestions. I'll contact the repairman you know first. If that doesn't work out, I'll take you up on borrowing your brother's old stove. In the meantime, I just hope the weather doesn't get any colder!

Analysis:
Mary has no heat. Her four friends give her many suggestions. She decides on one.

Pattern Review:

At least – the minimum, if nothing else, anyway,
The seats at the game were bad, but at least we could see the goals. Give me at least one pen. The job is not finished, but at least we started.

Work well together – a good combination, effective,
That pitcher and catcher work well together. The two new assistants work well together. This printer works well with my computer.

Reasonable – fair, not too expensive,
One dollar is a reasonable price for this notebook.

Asking me to work 12 hours a day was unreasonable. He's a reasonable man; he will listen to your complaints.

Contact – get in touch with, talk to, communicate with,
I will contact you if the schedule changes. Let's keep in contact. My son's teacher contacted me. It's not easy to contact anyone at that company.

Work out – be successful, solve a problem, produce a good result,
Their marriage did not work out; they got divorced. Changing the product name did not work out. Now that it's summer, everything should work out better. (Work out can mean doing exercise in a gym.)

Take someone up on – to accept an invitation or challenge,
If I am free, I will take you up on that golf invitation. I'll take you up on that offer you made to check my computer.

Meantime (meanwhile) –in the time between two happenings,
I will begin work next week. In the meantime I will practice my golf.

Challenge:
Repair a broken appliance or buy a new one?
a. How long should I keep my old car?
b. Which is better, to buy new or used items?
c. What do you buy at the Recycle Shop?

Problem with Mother-in-law:

A. Hi Mary. You look so sad today. What's the matter?

B. Hi Jane. It's just my mother-in-law. She visits us about once a week and goes through the house. She misses nothing. She checks the cupboards, the closets, and even the toilet.

A. How come you let her do that? Lock the doors. Keep her out. She has no right to check everything.

B. I know, but my husband does not want to upset her. He even gave her a key to our home. The worst part is listening to her complaining about how sloppy I am. It's depressing.

A. You have to put your foot down. Tell her she is welcome but do not let her inspect your home. She probably thinks you are not good enough for her son. Typical. (That is typical of mothers-in-law.)

B. You're right about that. The biggest problem is my husband has no backbone. He never confronts her. He is still a Mama's boy.
A. Change the lock on the door. If she does not like it -- too bad. You have to have some privacy. When you start acting tough, maybe your husband will get the message. Good luck.

B. I'll need it. But I am not going to put up with this any longer. Thanks for listening. Bye, I've got to go now. Talk to you later.

Analysis:
A lady has a problem with her mother-in-law and a spineless (weak) husband. His mother has a key to her son's home. Her friend gives her some advice and encourages her to stand up to her mother-in-law.

Pattern Practice:
 She goes through the house. –She checks everything. She goes through my pockets. She goes through my receipts and credit card statements.

Typical. – Many mothers-in-law are like that. She is like many other mothers-in-law. That's what people like that usually do.

He has no backbone. - He has no courage. He is weak.

If she doesn't like it – too bad. It's OK if she does not like it.

Put one's foot down. - Act tough, set limits. The children cannot come home when they like. I put my foot down and gave them a curfew.

Confront – ready to fight/argue, face a difficult situation,
I confronted him about his using my computer during lunch hour. He confronted his neighbor about the loud music.

He will get the message. - He will understand what you want. I opened all the windows when he started smoking. He got the message.

Put up with – endure, bear, suffer, condone, forgive, allow, let happen.
I will not put up with students coming late to class.

Challenge:
Typical mother-in-law problems. Or Good mothers-in- law.
 a. What are some reasons for changing jobs ?
 b. What you do if your child is being teased/bullied in school.
  c. Your idea of the perfect (ideal) husband or wife.

Problem with wife:

1. Hi Bill. You look down in the mouth today. What happened?

2. Hi Jon. It's the wife. She works as the secretary to the boss of the company. Every night she comes home later and later.

1. That's strange. You two always looked like the perfect couple. Does she have a good reason? What's her excuse?

2. It's overtime, a staff meeting, overseas' phone calls… I've heard them all. I know some of them are lies.

1. I hate to tell you, but I suspect she may be having an affair. But I am sure you know that.

2. She denies having an affair, but her boss got divorced recently, so it'd hard to believe her anymore. I don't know what to do.

1. Why don't you ask her to go to counseling with you? If she refuses, go alone. I hope you guys can stay together.

2. I'll ask her but I doubt she'll agree. She accuses me of being paranoid. It may be all over for us.

1. I'm sorry I can't help more. If there is anything I can do to help let me know.

Analysis:
Bill thinks (suspects) his wife is having an affair. His friend Jon is sympathetic but he cannot do much to help. All the evidence points to an affair.

Pattern Practice:

Look down in the mouth – look sad, look depressed,
He looks down in the mouth, he lost all his money gambling.

Evidence – what leads to proof. Police collect evidence of a crime.

Deny – say 'no' to an accusation (charge). He denied taking my pen.

Stay together – not get divorced. They stayed together for the children.

Paranoid –mental sickness where a person thinks he/she is being abused.
The paranoid man thought the mailman was going to arrest him.

Let me know – tell me, contact me. Let me know if you need help.

Challenge: a. An employee is stealing from the company.
b. A worker reads personal email during work.
c. Discuss international marriages.

Problem with Husband:

1. Hi Maria. Great to see you! Shopping without your husband?

2. Hi Jane. Nice to see you. I'm afraid my husband is not in great shape. He works overtime every day. He spends Saturdays sleeping and Sundays playing pachinko. He has no time for the family.

1. That's terrible. It must be the overwork. He is probably suffering from stress. Has he seen a doctor recently?

2. He doesn't want to get a checkup. He is putting on weight, so he knows what the doctor will tell him. But I am worried.

1. Can he change jobs or refuse to work so long? He can't keep this up. He is killing himself. He has got to slow down.

2. In this economy it is very hard to get a new job. Besides, he is not getting any younger. He would change if he could, but then he would lose his seniority and retirement benefits.

1. You are a great cook. So maybe you should both open up a restaurant. I bet it would be successful.

2. Maybe we should consider it. But with kids in school we feel it is better to have a steady income. I just hope I don't end up a widow!

Analysis:

Two friends meet and they talk about one woman's husband. Too much overtime is changing him for the worst. The friend offers advice but the friend's options are limited due to age and worries about money.

Pattern Practice:

Put on weight – gain weight… get fatter… get a spare tire…
He knows what the doctor will tell him.- I don't know where you live. She doesn't know what to buy. You know why I came. He knows how to play.
He can't keep this up.- He cannot continue. The runner's pace is too fast; he can't keep it up. He studied for 10 hours yesterday, but he can't keep that up.
He's not getting any younger.- He is getting old.

Challenge:
    Talk about a difficult new neighbor.
    a.   How to change jobs in a bad economy.
    b.   Your children are going to change high schools.
    c.   You are looking for a new hairdresser or barber.

Problems with People:

1. Excuse me Mr. Jones. I want to talk to you about parking. You may not realize it, but you often park in my space. My apartment number is 13. Spaces 13 and 14 have been assigned to me. I'd appreciate it if you would not park there anymore.

2. Well, Mr. Dokes, let me tell you something. In this apartment complex there are no designated parking spaces. It's a case of first come first served. If you don't like my parking in 13 or 14 that is too bad. That's your problem. I intend to park wherever I like, and you can do nothing about it. Now if you'll excuse me, I have a football game to watch.

1. Sorry to trouble you again Mr. Jones, but it seems I owe you an apology. According to the rental agreement, I park in 13 and you park in 14. I presume your agreement says the same. Thanks for your cooperation.

Analysis:

Mr. Dokes and Mr. Jones are neighbors. The former (Dokes) thinks he has the exclusive right to two parking spaces. Later he checks the rental agreement and realizes he has only one space. Mr. Jones is not likely to become more friendly.

Patterns Practice:

You may not realize it – you may be unaware – you may not know it.

Assigned- specially set aside by one in authority; appointed. This is my assigned seat. The coach assigned each player a number.

Appreciate – feel thankful for, feel gratitude for, would like, (know the value of) I'd appreciate it if you would do the dishes. I'd appreciate it if you would write this address in Japanese for me. I'd appreciate a cup of tea now. I appreciate your advice. (She appreciates good wine.)

 Designated- assigned, set aside. This train car is designated for women only. You may smoke only in the designated area. We have designated parking spaces. David Ortiz was the designated hitter for the Red Sox.

I owe you an apology – I wish to apologize. I owe you a debt of gratitude. - I need to say thanks to you. I owe you $10.00. I should pay back $10.00.

I presume- I believe something for a good reason. It's 3:00 PM, I presume you had lunch. I presume you went to the U.S. by plane.

Challenge :   Imagine a fight between neighbors.
a. Talk about ... a noisy neighbor...a barking dog...
b. Discuss loud music... rude children...confrontations
c. Are people basically honest?

Problem with a Machine:

1. Miss Ito, I need your help. There seems to be something wrong with this machine. I tried to make copies and all I get is noise. What's wrong with it?   I know you understand copiers. Please take a look at it.

2. Let me see. Have you checked the paper try? That looks OK. There is plenty of paper. Maybe it's out of toner (ink). Press that lever there, it opens the front. Ah, there's the problem. There are two pages stuck in there. When we remove them it will be OK.

1.Thank you Miss Ito. I don't know what I'd do without you. Don't ever leave this company. I can't run the machinery. If you ever try to leave, I'll make a copy of you first. Maybe we should clone you!

2.You are welcome. I am lucky I used to be the editor and publisher of our school newspaper. We did not have the latest equipment, so we learned a lot from machines that broke down often. But don't bother cloning me; my mother and brothers were always happy I did not have a twin sister!

Analysis:

The boss depends on Miss Ito to solve problems with the copier. He is friendly, appreciative (thankful), and humorous. Miss Ito explains how she obtained expertise with printers.

Challenge:
   Explain how to use a new copier.
   a. How to eat sushi…pizza…
   b. Why you need your GPS…
   c. Tour guide's job… to accept/not to accept tips…

Problem with a Company:

1. Good morning. How may I help you? Would you care for something to drink? How about tea or coffee?

2. No thanks. I just dropped in to clear up a slight problem. Last year we bought $5,000.00 worth of furniture from your company, and we paid by check – cashier's check. But every month we get an invoice demanding payment. I brought a copy of the canceled check with me. So I'd like an explanation.

1.Were all the demands signed by Don Felon? I see. Well, we are having a lot of trouble with this young man. About six months ago we fired him for embezzling funds. But it seems he copied some of our customers' files and took them with him. We are now in the process of filing charges against him. Could you bring in or mail in copies of the dunning notices he sent you? There will be a court case next month, and we can use these notices as evidence. I am glad you brought it to my attention. To show our appreciation, I will personally give you 10% off your next order. Just send it through me. Here's my business card.

Analysis:
A customer keeps getting billed for furniture he has paid for. The problem is a fired employee who is making trouble. A court case is pending so this harassment should end soon. The company offers the customer 10% off his next order.

Patterns Practice:

Dunning notices – demanding payment for what is owed.

We are in the process of …ing - in the middle of this action.
We are in the process of remodeling our kitchen. They are in
the process of moving. They are in the proccss of opening a
new store.

To file charges – to take someone to court. He will file
charge against the man who assaulted (hit) him.

Bring it to my attention – tell me about it – let me know.
Thanks for bringing that leak to my attention.

Challenge:
Someone stole your credit card and you are billed.
a. Received the wrong shipment…billed twice…
b. Your hotel room is not availablc…what they offer...
 c. You still receive the newspaper that you canceled.

Problem with the Boss:

1. Mr. O'Gowan, thank you for meeting with me. As you
know, recently my workload and my responsibilities have
increased. Especially with Bill out sick for such a long time.
So I thought this would be a good time to ask for a raise. It
has been two years since the last raise. I believe the company
can afford it.

2. I'm glad you came in Jack. Bill won't be coming back. He
has terminal cancer. Just keep it under your hat for now. So
we are going to combine the marketing and training
departments. I'd like you to run this new section. It will be a
new challenge, but I know you can handle it. Salary-wise I
will mean an extra $12,000.00 a year. How does that sound?

Analysis:
Jack feels that his extra work deserves extra salary. He will get more responsibility and also more wages.

Pattern Practice:

Afford – can do easily, able to buy, have enough money for, We can't afford to waste water. They can afford a long vacation. You can't afford to waste time. I can't afford a Ford so I drive a used car.

Terminal cancer- there is no hope of recovery. His illness is terminal.

Keep it under your hat- keep it a secret.-Don't tell anyone.

How does that sound? – What do you think of that? For your birthday we will go bowling, and then I will take you out to dine. How does that sound?

Challenge:

Explain why you are leaving the company.
a. Why you have to fire a worker.
b. Why workers will get a smaller bonus this year…
c .Your promotion has been decided.

Problem with an Employee:

1. Mary, I have to remind you of our company policy. There will be no smoking at your desk during work. The equipment you use is very sensitive. Cigarette ash will ruin it. Besides, other employees have complained about your smoking. They don't like second-hand smoke. You may take four smoke breaks a day, but smoke in the designated area. I think that is fair to you and to the company.

2. Thank you, Mr. Smith. I will follow company rules and do as you say. Four smoking breaks a day is quite sufficient. I will try to quit smoking after Christmas.

Analysis:

Mary does not realize how dangerous and unpopular her smoking is. The company sets up a smoking area which can be used four times a day. Mary is satisfied and promises to try to quit smoking later.

Pattern Practice:

Remind- helps one to remember. This place reminds me of home. Photos remind us of happy times. That billboard reminds me to turn here when I am going to the beach. My boss's way of speaking reminds me of my father.

Sensitive- easily damaged or hurt. Some machines are very sensitive. (Dust or dirt can break them.) People also are also sensitive. It is easy to hurt their feelings.

Ruin – to make no good. Spilled coffee ruined my shirt. Rain ruined our picnic.

Sufficient- enough. One hamburger is sufficient for most people.

Quit – stop doing, give up. He quit karate and took up judo. He quit his job and moved to Hokkaido. "Quit teasing your little brother." Quit smoking.

Challenge:
 One employee does not like to shower.
 a. Why we are starting drug testing…
 b. Too many pens disappearing from the workplace…
 c. Your boss is a micro manager…

Problem Finding my Way:

1. Excuse me. Could you help me? I am looking for Phoenix Street and Second Avenue. According to the map it should be here.

Certainly. Let me help you. You have an old map. Phoenix Street is now divided into east and west by the new expressway.

 Keep going along this street. When you get to the second traffic light take a right. Then go straight for about one kilometer. You will go under the expressway. When you pass the City Hall – you'll see it on your left – it's a red brick building- take the first left, and that will be Phoenix Street.

Second Avenue is either the second or third intersection. You can't miss it.
A Navy Bank is on the corner of Second Avenue and Phoenix Street.

1. Thank you for your help. I should have no trouble finding it now.

2. You're welcome. By the way, watch your speed around City Hall. There is usually a patrol car hiding there somewhere.

Analysis:
Confusing map. Good directions + easy to see landmark.

Challenge:
 Directions from here to your home.
 a.   Directions to an office within a school or hospital.
 b.   Directions on how to move files in the computer.
 c.   How to use a new phone.

Problem at a Restaurant:
1. How is your steak? It looks rare. I thought you ordered medium well done?

2. I did. This steak is terrible. It looks raw. I am not going to eat it. Someone made a mistake so I am sending it back. Waiter!

2A. What seems to be the matter? How can I help you?

2. This steak is rare. I ordered mine medium well-done. Please take it back and cook it, or give me what I ordered.

2A. Certainly. I am very sorry for the mix up. I will have the cook rush your order. While you are waiting, may I bring you both another cocktail -on the house?

2. That is a good idea. Two more dry martinis.2A. I will be right back. Thank you for your patience and understanding.

Analysis:

A patron at the restaurant gets his steak cooked incorrectly. The waiter apologizes and offers two drinks on the house.

Pattern Practice:

Steak can be ordered: well-done, medium well-done, medium, and rare. (Rare is almost raw, or cooked slightly!)

On the house – free from the owner of the restaurant. Because Japan won the Asia Cup, drinks were on the house. (The owner likes soccer.) This bottle of wine is on the house. (You are one of our best patrons (customers).

Challenge:

You get a bill for food ordered at the table next to you.
a. An auto mechanic fixed your brakes; you only wanted an oil change.
b. The store wants you to buy an extended warranty on your TV.
c. The taxi driver wants to charge for each one in your group.

Problem at a Restaurant II:
1. Even though we had a reservation, they kept us waiting 15 minutes. I hope the food is worth waiting for.

2. They certainly have quite an extensive menu. I think I'll try the steak. I haven't had steak in a while. How about you? What are you going to have?

1. I'm not a great meat eater. I think I'll get the grilled salmon, with mashed potatoes and coleslaw. Here's the waiter now.

3. Good evening gentlemen. Care for a drink before your meal?

2. No thanks. We are hungry and ready to order. My friend would like the grilled salmon with mashed potatoes and coleslaw. I'll have the steak -medium rare. I'd like rice, mushrooms, and a side order of onion rings…

1. How is your steak? It looks tasty.

2. It is not what I ordered. I am sending it back. This is well done. I wanted mine medium rare. Can you catch the waiter's eye?

3. What seems to be the matter? How can I help?

2. I wanted my steak medium rare. This is well done. It is actually burned.

3. I apologize for the mix up. I will bring you another one very shortly.
 While you are waiting can I bring you some drinks on the house?
1.No thanks. We have a meeting after dinner so we need to 100% sober .

2. If he keeps me waiting his tip will start shrinking. I like good service.

1. Here he is now. Maybe it's not his fault. Don't get him a hard time.

2. I just hope he got it right this time. I'm starving.

Analysis:

What two friends order and why. Incorrect order returned. Bad service usually means a smaller tip.

Pattern Practice:
Side order- extra order that is not part of the meal selected.
Catch someone's eye – get his/her attention. (Used often in restaurants.)
Don't give him a hard time- Go easy on him. - Don't treat him harshly.

Challenge:

The repair shop tries to give you back the wrong watch.
 a. Order food at an expensive restaurant.
 b. Phone to have a pizza delivered.
 c. Make a phone call to praise a worker.

Eating Out- No Problem

1. What are you cooking (making) for dinner tonight?   I hope it's fish. You know I love fish.

2. I have a better idea. Why don't we eat out for a change? I'm tired of cooking every night. Besides, it's Kemiko's birthday today.

1. Thanks for remembering! That sounds like a great idea. Why didn't I think of that? Where will we go? Tokyo is full of good restaurants. Let's go to that new Korean restaurant. I heard they serve great steak there. We haven't had Korean food in ages. (...in a long time.) We can get there in 10 minutes.

2. No, we can't go there. I have an interview tomorrow, and I don't want to smell of garlic. If I didn't have the interview I would be happy to go there. There must be other places we can go to.

1. Why don't we go to the new sushi place near the station? We all like sushi, and prices are reasonable.

2. That place is always crowded on Tuesdays. You know I hate waiting. How about the restaurant near Shinjuku station? They have a great variety of Western & Japanese food. We have not been there since it opened. What do you think Kemiko?

3. That's fine with me. If you tell them it's my birthday, I get free dessert. Do we need to make a reservation?

2. Just phone and ask do we need one. It's usually not so crowded on Tuesdays. While you are at it, how about calling a taxi? I don't want your father to drink and drive. Let me get ready. I won't be long.   -125-

1. I am fine the way I am. I'll just put on a jacket. Kemiko are you going to go there in your school uniform?

3. Of course not. I am changing too. I have to wait until Mom is finished. We could do with another bathroom in this house.

1.It's OK. I am used to waiting. Take your time. I will read 'War and Peace' while I am waiting for you ladies.

2. Here we are. Where do you want to sit? We're lucky it's not crowded tonight. 1. How about over there?

3. Let's sit here in the no- smoking section. If my clothes smell of smoke my friends will think I have started smoking. Here is fine.

4. Good evening. My name is Leo. I will be your waiter tonight. Can I get you some drinks while you are checking the menu?

1. How about a martini for you, a virgin margarita for Kemiko, and I'll have a highball – Scotch on the rocks. Is that OK with everyone?

2. No problem, as long as you make my martini with gin not vodka. I don't like to see Kemiko drinking margaritas, but I guess it's OK since there is no alcohol in it.

4. I will get the drinks right away while you check the menu.

3. This is quite a large menu. Everything looks so good, I don't know what to order. What are you going to get Papa? (Dad).

1. I think I'll have the steak. Recently, I never eat much meat. How about you?

2. I'm going to get the lobster. We never cook them at home. But the swordfish steak looks good too. Maybe I should get that? How about you Kemiko? Did you decide? (Have you decided yet?)

3. I'm getting the roast beef dinner with a side order of onion rings. I'm getting dessert too. Lunch in school today was terrible. I hardly ate any of it. Here's our waiter. Let's order. I'm starving.

4. Here are your drinks and are you ready to order now?

2. Yes, I will have the swordfish steak dinner. But I'd like to change the vegetable. Can I get broccoli instead of mushrooms? And I'll have the mashed potatoes instead of French fries.

1. Let me have the sirloin steak - medium well done. With that I'd like green peas, mushrooms, and rice instead of potatoes. Kemiko?

3. Just bring me the roast beef dinner with a side order of onion rings. Can I get soup instead of salad?

4. Certainly. If you wish you can have both. The salad bar is over there. Just help yourself. What kind of soup would you like?

3. I'll have the split pea soup. Don't bring me any crackers with the soup. I want to save room for dessert.

4. Let me repeat your orders just to make sure. Swordfish steak with broccoli and mashed potatoes for the lady. And for the gentleman, sirloin steak, medium well- done, with peas, mushrooms, and rice.

And for the young lady, split pea soup, along with the roast beef dinner which includes carrots and parsnips, and a side order of onion rings. Would you like another round of drinks?

1. No, thank you. We will check out the salad bar. …

2. How is your roast beef, Kemiko, it looks delicious.

3. It is not great. It has too much fat. But the onion rings are out of this world. Try one. Mom, ask for the recipe.

2. How is the swordfish?

1. It's very tasty. The cheese sauce on the broccoli is excellent. How's your steak?

2. It's like leather! I can't chew it. I'm afraid I'll break my jaw. I think I'll send it back. It is well- done and I asked for medium. **OR** It is very tasty. I am glad I ordered it. It is **so** tender it melts in my mouth. Why don't you try a piece?

4. How is everything? Would you like to order anything else?

2. Everything is fine. My husband and I will have coffee after the meal. No dessert. Kemiko?

3. As it's my birthday today, I'll have apple pie and ice cream. Please heat up the apple pie first.

4. Coffee and dessert coming right up. The dessert is on the house as it is your birthday. Can I get you an after dinner drink?

1. No thank you, coffee will be fine.

2. The service was excellent tonight. Give him a good tip, he deserves it.

1. How much should I leave? Oh the tax is 8.5%, so I'll just double it.

Analysis:

 Father, mother & daughter decide to eat out on daughter's birthday. They order aperitifs (before dinner drinks) and are happy with the service.

Pattern Practice:

For a change - something different. Let's go by bus for a change, we always go by train. I always eat rice ; I'm going to eat potatoes for a change.

Tired of …ing- do something too often and dislike it. I'm tired of cooking; let's eat out. I'm tired of going by train; I need a car. I'm tired of studying for tests.

In ages- for a long time. I haven't played tennis in ages. She hasn't seen her son in ages. I have not been to Ireland in ages.

Fine with me- OK/it is all right for me. For shopping, anytime is fine with me.

Be long- a long time. I won't be long, I'm almost ready. Hurry up, don't be long.

Could do with- would like, want. I could do with a cup of tea. We could do with more workers. This room could do with a new coat of paint.

To be used to –ing - it is easy. I am used to driving in the city. He is used to working nights. They are used to commuting by train.

Take your time – go slowly, no rush. Take your time we are not in a hurry.

Instead of – in place of. I drink tea instead of coffee. He will come Monday instead of Saturday. You can drive instead of me.

How about –ing = Why don't you v. =you should v. For suggestions/advice. How about buying a new car? How about taking a nap?

To make sure- to be certain. Let me check the gas to make sure it's off. Make sure you have your passport. I'll check to door to make sure it is locked.

Out of this world- excellent, great. The colors of the foliage were out of this world. The service was out of this world.

Hardly – almost not. I can hardly hear you, speak louder. I could hardly see the game. The box was so heavy I could hardly lift it.

Deserve- should get by right. That student gets 100 in all her tests; she deserves an 'A'. He was speeding so he deserves to pay a big fine.

As long as- since, because. As long as you're going shopping, please buy me a pen. As long as you driving home let me go with you.

Challenge:
Let's go river rafting ...sailing ... skiing.)
a. Buying a new electrical appliance.
b. Planning a surprise birthday party for a family member.
a. Wedding anniversary party for your parents.

Problem with New Year's Resolutions:

1. Hi, Jon, Happy New Year. I hope this will be a super year for both of us.

2. Happy New Year to you too Mary. I am sure it will be a great year. You always make New Year resolutions. Did you make any this year?

 1. Of course. But I have a hard time following through. This year I mean to lower my blood pressure and lose 5 kilograms. So far I have exercised only one day, and I gained almost one kilo.

2. I think I can help you. Did you write down your resolutions and post them on the refrigerator? That helps. Also, can you invite a friend to do exercise with you? That always helps.

1. No, I just try to do things myself but I get discouraged so easily. Maybe I should do what you suggest. How do you keep your resolutions?

2. I am like a kid. I add rewards. When I do what I planned, I reward myself. Nothing spectacular, just a piece of candy or a cookie.

1. Do you punish yourself if you fail? What do you do then?

2. Yes, as a matter of fact I do. If I don't exercise, I cut out all snacks for two days. I also put a big red X on my refrigerator. Then every day I keep my resolution, I color a little of the X black. When it's all black, I feel good.

1. Maybe I should try that. But today I am just going to walk five kilometers instead of jogging.

2. That's the spirit Mary. I will join you. I need to lose a few kilos too. Let's try power walking. It's fun and a great way to keep fit.

Analysis:

Two friends discuss New Year's resolutions. Mary feels like a failure, so Jon helps with some practical advice.

Patterns Practice:

Follow through- to do what one promised or planned. The city promised to put in a new traffic light here, but they never followed through.

So far – up to now. I began reading the book. So far I have read only two pages. (So far so good =everything has gone fine up to now.)

Nothing spectacular – something ordinary, not special. He took the family out to eat. Nothing spectacular, they just went to a local restaurant.

Cut out – give up, quit doing/eating/drinking. I cut out eating ice cream.

That's the spirit. - I like your courage.

Challenge:
The best way to lose weight.
 a. How to learn a new language.
 b. How to finish Christmas shopping early.
 c. How to make friends in a new neighborhood.

**HINT: How to begin a conversation with someone you do
not know.** Be friendly. Smile. Talk about something neutral
that is present. Make a comment first. Do not ask personal
questions. Do not give a lot of information about yourself.
The following four conversations will give you an example.

To Begin a Conversation with a Stranger:

1. Excuse me, but I see you are using an electronic book. I
am thinking about buying one. What do you think of it?

2. It is very easy to use. I find it easy to read. It is not hard to
change the size of the print. So if I forget my glasses I can
still use it.

1. I am more of a text person. I like to read print and turn the
pages myself.
I think I could never get used to an electronic device like that.

2. Here, why don't you read a couple of pages and see what
you think of it. …

1. It's not as strange as I thought. I may buy one or drop a
few hints before Father's Day. Thanks for letting me try it.

2. You're welcome. Glad you liked it.

Analysis:

Seeing a person using an electronic reading device arouses the speaker's curiosity and interest. He gets information and a chance to use it for a short time. He may get one later.

Pattern Practice:

I am thinking about buying a car. She is thinking about moving to Osaka. We are thinking of selling our home. I was thinking about taking up golf.

It is easy to use… hard to use… easy to speak …easy to cook...hard to write…easy to fix…easy to read… hard to find, easy to do, hard to do.

Find – to know from experience. I find Japanese difficult. She finds English easy. We found Tokyo crowded. They found Kyoto beautiful.
I find sushi tasty. I found London very expensive.

Get used to ..ing – (am used to ..ing) find something easy due to doing it many times. She is used to living in America now. I am used to driving on the left side of the road. We are used to getting up early. I'm used to drinking green tea now.

Used to v. - did once but don't do it anymore. I used to live in Osaka.

In America, I used to drive on the right.
She used to work in Kyoto. My father used to smoke. We used to eat American food. She used to be a teacher.

 See what you think of it – check it out, see for yourself. This is the new computer; see what you think of it.

Challenge:
  What I'd like for my birthday
   A. Why I need a Smart phone…(I- phone)
   b. Magazine subscription…
   c. Explain why your new camera makes you happy.

To Begin a Conversation: II

1. Excuse me, I see you are reading a soccer magazine. Do you happen to know who won between Manchester United and Manchester City? I am a big EPL fan. (EPL -English Premier League)

 2. Sorry, I don't know the score, but I can check it for you on my 'Smartphone'. Let me see… here it is, Man U won 3-2. Are you a Man U. fan (supporter)?

1. Yes, I am. I spent a summer in Manchester when I was a little boy. I got Ryan Giggs' autograph. So I got hooked on Man U.

2. They always manage to have a strong team. I guess they have a great organization.

1. And a great coach. Alex Ferguson really develops players. They all really like him. By the way, which team do you like?

2. I'm from Osaka so I am just interested in Osaka teams. One of my friends has a brother playing for Gamba, so we can always get tickets. Do you like the J League?

1. I watch it sometimes. I especially like to see Endo playing. He seems to have a great understanding of the game.

2. He plays for the national team also. He is one of the best in Japan. Luckily he plays for Osaka Gamba, so I can watch him often.

1. This is my station. Again thanks for your help. I appreciate it.

2. You're welcome. Glad to help.

Analysis:
A soccer magazine helps to initiate this conversation. Both men love soccer. One man supports Osaka Gamba F.C.; the other is a Manchester United fan for a good reason.

Pattern Practice:

I got hooked on soccer-I got to love it very much. She is hooked on pop music. Even my kids are hooked on skiing. They're hooked on camping.

Appreciate – to feel grateful for, to feel thankful for. I appreciate your help. I appreciate your kindness. I appreciate your helping me.

Seems- it looks like. My mother seems to enjoy visiting Las Vegas. The children seem to enjoy soccer more than video games. It seems to rain more in Kawasaki than in Tokyo. There seems to be a problem with the keyboard.

Spend – use time or money.
I spend 8 hours sleeping. She spent $200.00 on shoes. He spends 40 hours working. We spent a fortune on gasoline. I spent a day in Kyoto.

Challenge:

Mention somewhere worth visiting in your city.
a. You notice someone wearing your alma mater's shirt …
b. Share an interest in photography…
c. Which local food is worth trying …

Conversation (at the supermarket):

1. There are long lines at the cashiers' today. I hope they are fast and efficient. Waiting is not one of my virtues.

2. I know what you mean. But usually they are quite fast. I chose this line because the cashier is a little older. She should have more experience.

1. They have self-check-out but I seldom use it. Usually I mess it up and it takes longer than going to a cashier. Then I also use coupons.

2. I never use coupons; I am too lazy to cut them out. But I do bring a calculator.

1. A calculator? You don't need a calculator. The cashier has one.

2. Yeah, but sometimes the price marked on the item is not the one they ring up. So I like to keep them honest.

1. I never thought of that. I don't even keep my receipts. Maybe I should be more careful. Mistakes can happen.

2. You can bet on it. Last week my calculator saved me $5.00. It was a genuine mistake. Someone forgot to program the cash register with the correct price. They forgot the item was on sale.

1. Thanks for the tip. I will bring one in future. You're next. This lady is quite fast. I am glad we did not change lines.

2. Murphy's Law: If you change lines, the line you leave goes faster.

1. Nice talking with you. Maybe I'll see you here again.

2. With a calculator!

Analysis:
Waiting in line for a cashier at the supermarket leads to an interesting conversation. It includes the reason why the customer chose that line, and why one customer brings a calculator when shopping.

Pattern Practice:

Efficient- can do things well and fast. My wife is efficient.

Cashiers- at the check-out stations, -they take your cash (payment),

Waiting is not one of my virtues- I don't like waiting.

Patience is not one of his virtues- He is impatient.

I know what you mean – I empathize with you. I understand how you feel.

'Murphy's Law: 'Everything that can go wrong will go wrong at the most inconvenient time.' (E.g. You are late leaving home, your shoelaces break and you forget your car keys. Or: The person who falls asleep first is the loudest snorer.)

Challenge: Why you use/do not use coupons.
  a. Conversation about car licenses & insurance.
  b. Pickpockets - overseas tourist traps.
  c. How to save money when traveling.

The Scenery:

A. Excuse me, but do you know the name of that river? I don't remember ever seeing it before. It looks so beautiful.

B. I believe it is the Shinano River. It is the longest river in Japan. It flows north- northeast from the Japan Alps.

A. In spring it must be very beautiful. I love the sound of its name. It reminds me of Shenandoah in Virginia. How long it is?

B. It is over 300 kilometers. But as this is snow country it sometime floods. But it is beautiful. You can get a better picture of it when we stop at the next station.

A. I will definitely be back here in spring. This scenery has to be seen to be believed. It is breath taking. I bet some of these views are on many calendars.

Analysis: 1. What is the name of the river?
            2. Answers – facts
            3. More questions
            4. Photo ops-. where to get the best ones.

Challenge:
  Tokyo Sky Tree compared with Tokyo Tower…..questions
  a. What one should do at a Japanese/American wedding.
  b. Where one should visit in Japan/America + reasons.
  c. Explain some photos or postcards from your last trip.

Pattern Practice:

Reminds – helps me to remember. That school reminds me of my youth.

Definitely – surely, certainly, without a doubt.
I will definitely try 'natto' before I leave Japan. ('Natto' is fermented beans.)

It has to be seen to be believed. It is extremely beautiful. Incredible.

Office Gossip:

1. Did you hear the latest? Bill asked Mary to go out with him. She's on cloud nine. They are going to go dancing this weekend.

2. Bill and Mary? It will never last. Bill has dated almost all the girls in this company. Don't let those good looks fool you. He's as phony as a three-dollar bill.

1. Well, I like him. I'm a little jealous. He never asked me to go out with him. He's always so optimistic and cheerful, besides, he has a great sense of humor. Of course he's not getting any younger. Maybe he is ready to settle down. I wish them luck.

2. I don't really dislike him, but I don't trust him. He was engaged twice before. Granted he's funny, but he's not good at making decisions.

1. Mary will straighten him out. She is very strong-willed, and has a stubborn streak. Maybe opposites do attract! Besides, Mary is no spring chicken.

2. I bet you one dinner Mary dumps him after one date. This won't last.

1. I'll take you up on that. I am sure I will win. They are both the wrong side of 30. Don't let Mary know you are betting on her love life!

Analysis:
This office conversation shows us how two girls view an office romance. Bill's virtues and vices are clearly mentioned. They bet one dinner on the likelihood it won't last.

Pattern Practice:

Did you hear the latest? Do you know the latest news, gossip, rumors?

She's on cloud nine.- She's very happy. –She's walking on air.

He's phony- He is not to be trusted. (Two-faced).

He's not getting any younger. He is getting old. It is time to settle down.

Settle down – become more serious and get married.

Opposites attract- people with different personalities get married. (A shy girl may marry a very outgoing man, or vice versa.)

 She is no spring chicken. She is not young.
Granted he's funny- I agree with you that he is funny. I admit. (But I don't agree with everything else you said.) Granted this is the longest way, but the traffic moves faster than on the short cut.   -141-

Stubborn streak- she tends to have a strong will and does not change her mind quickly. My father has a stubborn streak. He will never vote for a young politician.

She will dump him.- She will end the relationship. They went steady for a few months, then she dumped him. He dumped her in favor of a younger lady.

The wrong side of thirty.- They are over thirty years of age.

I'll take you up on it. - I will accept the challenge.

Challenge:
What you think of Internet Dating Services
  a. The movie star I'd like to marry…
  b. I read/never read my horoscope…
  c. Movies worth/not worth watching

Idioms using part of the body:

I had butterflies in my stomach during the interview. (I was very nervous.) She has a sweet tooth. (She likes sweet food.) He's a pain in the neck. (He's hard to get along with.) He has sticky fingers. (He steals.) I have a heavy (lead) foot. (I tend to drive very fast.) She came in with her nose in the air. (She's very proud/stuck up.) She has an eye for beauty. (She is a good judge of beautiful things.) She has an ear for music. (She understands music well.) Let's play it by ear. (Let's not have a schedule but just decide on the spot what to do or where to go next.) I can't stomach violence. (I don't like violence.)
He is very nosy. (He is very curious about other people's lives.) I'd give my right arm to meet Ichiro. (I really would love to meet him.) That mansion cost an arm and a leg. (It was very expensive.) He's only pulling your leg. (He's only joking.)They work hand in glove.

(They cooperate in two related businesses; e.g. a car insurance agent and a car repair facility.) He is two-faced. (He is sly and can't be trusted.) He has a finger in many pies. (He has many business interests.) She has a big mouth. (She talks too much and too freely.) He has his head in the clouds. (He is not very practical.) This is back-breaking work. (It is very hard work.) The company will foot the bill. (The company will pay.) I put my foot in my mouth. (I said something I regret saying.) I made it by the skin of my teeth. (I just made it. I barely succeeded. I was just in time.) He missed by a hair. (He missed by a very small margin.) He's very tight-fisted. (He is stingy, mean, does not give away any money.) If you steal you have to face the consequences. (You have to suffer punishment for what you do wrong.) My hair stood on end. (I was very scared.) I was sweating bullets. (I was very nervous.)

"Break a leg." (A wish for success for actors and actresses.) That was a close shave. (A danger that just missed or did not happen.) Those two don't see eye to eye. (They do not agree with each other.) There's more than meets the eye in that agreement. (There are some secrets involved in that deal.) To be a kindergarten teacher you need eyes in the back of your head. (K teachers have to be very careful and observant.) Keep an eye on the baby while I go shopping. (Take care of the baby.) When the boss married his secretary it raised eyebrows. (Everyone was surprised.) She took the job with eyes wide open. (She knew what she was doing.) The shoplifter just walked out with the stolen goods and never batted an eyelid. (He was cool and confident.) He lives hand to mouth. (He is very poor.) You took the words right out of my mouth. (You said exactly what I was going to say.) Students paid lip service to many of the rules. (They ignored them.) When Santa came in the kids were all eyes. (They were watching very carefully.) They were all ears waiting to find out who won the raffle. (They were all listening carefully.)

The Libyan regime is on its last legs. (It is weak and ready to collapse.) The citizens were up in arms about the new tax. (They opposed it strongly.) When I go to Las Vegas I don't chance my arm. (I don't take risks or gamble.)
The news of my bonus was music to my ears. (It made me very happy.) The choice of taking my bonus now or ten years from now was a no brainer. (It was easy to decide.)
After work, she lets her hair down. (She has a very good time.) The boss must put his money where his mouth is. (He must do what he promised or talked about.) The name of the product is on the tip of my tongue. (I just cannot think of the name right now.) My plea for volunteers fell on deaf ears. (No one volunteered.) The children need more elbow room. (They need more space.) Before I travel, I want to pick your brains. (I want to avail of your experience and expertise.) He's all brawn and no brain. (He is strong but not clever.) Off the top of my head, I'd say there are 12 million people in Tokyo. (It is just an educated guess, not exact.) He has a swelled head now just because he got a 100 in the test. (He is very proud.) Don't bite the hand that feeds you. (Be grateful to those who support you.) I heard it first hand that we are moving next year. (I heard it directly from the boss.) She knows the city like the back of her hand. (She knows it well.) I wash my hands of the PTA. (I will have nothing more to do with the PTA.) In some countries you have to grease the palms of officials to get what you need. (You have to bribe them.) Idle hands tempt the devil. (If (young) people are not doing something useful, they may do bad things.) You are a sight for sore eyes. (I am happy to see you.) I have a bone to pick with you. (I want to discuss something with you.) She turned up her nose at my suggestion. (She rejected it.) The demonstration got out of hand. (It developed into a riot or it was uncontrolled.) She goes around with a chip on her shoulder. (She is always unhappy because of some slight she suffered in the past.) It was hard to keep a straight face. (It was hard to keep from laughing.)

His poker face fooled everyone. (He tricked all by not showing any emotion.) In college, keep your nose clean. (Do not get into trouble.) It's no skin off my nose. (It does not affect me at all.) You can't put an old head on young shoulders. (You cannot expect young people to be mature.) He stabbed his fellow workers in the back. (He proved to be untrustworthy.) Her heart is in the right place. (She means well.)

Discussion Scenarios:

Listening, Taking Action, Taking Sides, Imagining Possibilities, Figuring Out Solutions, , Identifying Causes, Imagining Other Effects, Expressing Feelings, Compromising, Recalling Similar Experiences, etc.

The students listen to/read each scenario and explain what the conversation is about. Then they have to give reasons for or against any action they would like to take. They can mention feelings, contradictions, values, possible outcomes, possible solutions, advice, related problems, experience, and other possible problems. The students can role play being the opponent (against) or proponent (for) each argument. Some topics will interest teens, others may have to be made age appropriate.

1."That mother is beating her child. She is using her hand to hit her infant. She is out of control. I will call the police. That is not right. She will injure the child."
What is happening? Who is talking? What kind of person is she/he? What would you do in that case? Should he/she get involved?

2. "Look ! I found a wallet on the road. It has $50.00 in it. This is my lucky day. Let's go to the movies and later to a coffee shop. My treat."
What happened? What kind of person is the finder? What would you do if he invited you?

3."It's raining. If we walk home we will get wet. I will ruin my new dress/suit. If we go by taxi we will have no money left to buy a present for mother on Mother's Day. What should we do?" The best solution?" (Children's topic).

4.A" That pit bull coming toward us looks mean. Maybe we should call the police. He may attack someone." B: " It's OK. I am good with animals. I will catch him." What is going on here? What is the danger? What is the speaker going to do? What may happen? What would you do?

5."We each have only $5.00 for lunch. If we go to The Café we can buy only food and no drinks. If we go to The Bistro we will have enough money for drinks but no food. What should we do?" (Children's problem)
What is the problem? How much money do they have? How will they find the answer to this problem (dilemma)? What would you do?

 6. "Hi Mary. I have great news. My parents said I could get a pet. But I don't know what to do. I like cats but my sister is allergic to cats. She is only three years old. I can't make up my mind." (Pre-teen problem)
What will this girl do? What should she do? What would yo

7."For Christmas I got new gloves. They were very expensive. I lost one on my way to school. I didn't tell my Mom yet. If I tell her she will get angry at me. What will I do?" (Teen problem) What happened? What is the best solution? What would you do?

8." I love red hair. I want to dye my hair red. All my friends have red hair. If I dye mine, Mom threatened (promised) to cut it off. What should I do?" (Teen problem)
What is this student's problem? What kind of mother does she/he have? What should she do? What would you do?

9. "During the summer I want to work part time. My parents want me to go to summer school for biology. You know I failed it last term. But if I don't work I won't be able to buy a motorbike in September. What should I do?"(Teen)
What is the problem? What kind of student is he/she? What should he do? What would you do?

11. Kemiko is such a nice girl. I don't know how to talk to her about her weight. She is always eating snacks. Everyone is laughing at her. How can we help her to lose weight?"
What is the problem? Why is there a problem? What should her friends do? What would you do? Is it really your business to worry about a friend's weight?

12. "Look Bill ! There is our friend J. shoplifting. That is not right. He knows better. That is stealing. What will we do? If we call the police he will never get into a good university as he will have a criminal record. We must do something."
What is the problem? Is it really a problem? How far should friendship go? What should they do? Is shoplifting such a terrible crime? What would you do?

13. "I have a problem at work. My boss keeps giving me lots of work because he knows I can do it. Now it is taking up too much of my time. If I ask for less work, I am afraid I may not get a promotion that is coming up. What should I do?"
What is the problem? Is it the Peter Principle? How is it affecting your family? What is one solution? What would you do?

14."The group of friends I hang out with love bowling. I go along because there is one boy (girl) in the group that I like. But I hate bowling. What should I do?" What is the problem? Is it a very small problem? Will it go away with time? What should she (he) do? What would you do?

15."John and Mary were collecting donations for the earthquake victims. They spent six weekends in front of the station. They got a lot of money. Last week John took Mary out to a nightclub and dinner. They both bought new clothes. Maybe they are stealing donations? Is this a real problem? How can we know for sure? Is this a case of MYOB? Should friends be nosy? What would you do?

16."Our friend Jill has a problem. She graduated from high school and was accepted into both her father's and mother's alma maters. She does not know which one to choose. She can't please both her parents."
What should Jill do? What advice would you give her? If you were Jill what would you do?

17."The SAT results came in yesterday. J got full marks- 100% on the test, but I know he cheated. He stole a copy of the test the night before. I overheard him boasting about it to his girlfriend. What can I do?" What is the problem? Did J really cheat? Can it be proved? What should she do? What would you do?

18. "My neighbor Bill is dishonest. He stopped working for a building company. (construction co.) He said he had strained his back. He pretends it is painful just to get worker's compensation. Every night he works part time unloading trucks at the supermarket. I feel he is ripping off the government. What should I do?" What is the problem? No one is being injured so maybe there is no problem? What should he/she do? What would you do?

19."Our teacher is strange. He brings a big jug (container) of orange juice to the classroom every day. But it is not really OJ. It is 50% vodka. He can teach OK, but I think he is an alcoholic. What should we do?" What is the problem? Is it really a problem? What should they do? What would you do?

20."You know Mary is our good friend. Well, yesterday I saw her father hugging and kissing a lady in the park. It was not her mother. I felt terrible. I don't know what to do."
What is the problem? Is it really a problem? Should he/she mind her own business? Whom should he/she tell? What would you do? If you were Mary would you like to be told? The best solution?

21.Our friends Bill and Mary (siblings) have a problem. They are both working and wish to get married soon. But their parents need money to retire and pay medical bills. They depend on Bill & Mary to help them.
What is the problem? What should they do? What advice would you give them? What would you do if you were in their shoes?

22. A."Oh, look at that poor homeless man. I pity him. Maybe he needs food. I'll give him some money to buy a sandwich and a drink."
B. "Are you kidding? He is drunk or on drugs. If you give him money he will spend it on booze. Let's keep on walking."
What is the situation? Is A or B correct? What would you do?

23."The innkeeper said they have only one room vacant. We can stay there for half price. The room is supposed to be haunted. That's why it is vacant and cheap. What do you want to do?" What is the problem? What would you do? Do you believe in ghosts?

24." I need your advice Jon. I found out my daughter's secret password and I read all her emails. She gets mail from many boys. I want to protect her so I must know what is going on. But I feel terrible sneaky."
Is this right? Is it OK for Mom/Dad to read their minor children's emails?

25.”We found a beautiful dog last month. Its leg was broken so we took it to the vet. It was very expensive to get it fixed. I know where the owner lives. But if we give it back, it will be treated cruelly again. So we decided to keep the dog.”
Is this OK? What is the crux of the problem? What should they do? What would you do?

26.”I'm getting married next month, but I have a big dilemma. You know my parents are divorced. If I invite both of them, they will have a big fight (row), and ruin my wedding. If I invite only one, it will ruin my relationship with the other one. What should I do?”
What is the problem? What should she do? What would you do?

27.”You know my brother is crazy about photography. Well, he secretly takes photos of the girl next door when she is sun bathing nude in her garden. Then he posts them on the Internet using a fake name. What should I do?”
What is the problem? Is it a privacy issue? Should she tell the police?

28. “Our company is very big but recently we have been losing a lot of money. I know some employees are stealing pens, pencils, and paper every day. What should I do? If I report them they may get fired.”
What is the problem? What should she/he do? What would you do?

29.”My brother is a gardener and he also cuts a lot of grass for people. But he always exaggerates the size of the gardens by including the area of the house in each estimate. The older people never notice and don't complain. I know I should do something, but my brother helps me out financially.”
What should she do? What is the problem? What would you do?

30.”You know Maria? Well, recently she is always half-joking about killing herself. It scares me. I don't know what is going through her mind. Maybe we should do something?” Is this really a problem? Is it just a joke? Is Maria's friend worrying too much? What should she do? What would you do?

31. My cousin Jon is quite a business man. He takes old bikes from the bicycle parking lot at the station. He cleans them up, paints them, and sells them on Ebay. I think that is not right. What do you think?
What is the problem? Is it stealing? (If he doesn't take them, they just rust.) So maybe it is OK?

32.”My friend Kemiko is quite a shopper. She buys everything at a discount. When there is a sale on, she switches the tags on the clothes. She saves a lot of money. That's how she bought this jacket for me.”Is there a problem? What should Kemiko's friend do? What would you do? What should she do with the jacket?

33.“My friend works at an Old Folks Home. The work is hard but she likes the 'benefits'. The old people don't notice when she helps herself to their snacks, watches, and jewelry. Most of them have no living relatives so it is not really stealing.”
Is it stealing? Maybe she is being underpaid? If she does not take the stuff, then someone else will. So maybe it is OK? What do you think?

34.”My son is doing his thesis for graduation now. He is just translating one that was done in Gaelic (Irish) by some Irish student in Dublin. The U.S. university will never find out. It's no big deal. 'Is it a big deal? Should you tell on him? What should you do/say?

35."Mary is dating two young men now. She said she will marry the one with the most money. I know one of them. He is just going to borrow money from the bank to impress her, and then give it back after the wedding. Should I tell Mary?"
Is this really a problem? Is it a case of MYOB? What should Mary's friend do? What would you do?

36."It is tax time again. I pay too much in taxes. So this year I am not mentioning my part time job. Besides, they pay me in cash. The IRS (Tax Office) will never find out."
Is this OK? Should you pay more taxes? Is it a problem? Doesn't everyone do the same thing?

37.."I am getting married next month. There is one little problem. My fiancee's parents think I graduated from Yale. I told them that to impress them. They are big on education. So at the wedding reception I want you to be my Yale classmate. OK?"Is this OK? Is it a lie? Will you go along with your friend's idea? What is the best solution? What would you do?

38."As you know my father is very sick in hospital. He has incurable cancer. So we told the doctors and nurses just to make sure he is comfortable; we don't want any extra expenses. You know how it is."
Could this be a real live situation? In your family? Is it practical or mean? If you were dying how would you feel? Should they spend more money on their father?

39."Do you know that we are the only family paying for school lunch? All the other families lie about their salaries. Their kids eat for free. It's not fair. I am going to do something about it."
Is she/he correct? What should she do? What would you do? Maybe all her neighbors will hate her and boycott her? What can she do?

40."My friend Kate is a popular baby sitter. She has a little problem with alcohol (booze). She helps herself to whiskey or vodka when the children go to sleep. I am worried about the children. What if something bad happened?"What should Kate's friend do? What if she gets drunk and there is a fire? What if she falls asleep? Should the parents be told? What would you do?

41. "My brother Jack is a bartender. (He mixes drinks for people.) When customers order an expensive brand of sake or vodka, he gives it to them only for the first drink. Then he substitutes a cheaper brand but the customers never notice it. But he charges them for the expensive stuff. Is that OK? What should you do? Maybe he will be found out?

42."Bill works with me in the same office. The owner of our small company loves to play golf. So when he leaves early, Bill also leaves early. I don't know what to do? "What should Bill's friend do? Is this cheating? What would you do?

43. "Mary's mother is a cashier at the supermarket. She knows I am Mary's best friend. If I don't go to her register she gets upset. But if I go to her register she only charges me for half the things I buy. "What should Mary's friend do? Is this OK? What would you do?

44. "My grandpa is very kind. He lives in the same town as we do. Every time we visit him he gives us money. My sister sometimes visits him two or three times a week. Grandpa is losing his memory so he gives her money each time. I think this is not right."(Teen) Is it OK? Should she be stopped? What would you do? Give reasons for and against.

45.”There is a mean old lady living next door to us. She has a big apple tree but she never picks the apples. As it is near our garden we help ourselves to most of the apples. If we don't take them, they will just rot. Is that a problem?” What do you think? Is it stealing? Is there any way to compensate the old lady? What would you do?

46. Liz is the manager of a pizza restaurant. The local under-12 soccer team wants her to sponsor the team. It will cost her at least $500.00. Should she do it? What are the pros and cons?

47. Your best friend is eloping with a drug addict tonight. You 'know' that this marriage is never going to succeed. What should you do? Should you be concerned?

48. Your best friend in high school is pregnant. No one else knows. Your father is a gynecologist who performs abortions. You know he will help her but you do not agree with abortions. What would you advise her? Should you inform some adults?

49. You were cleaning up the attic and found some old papers in a box. They are your adoption papers. You are shocked and surprised. What should you do? Pretend you never found them? Confront (question) the parents who raised you? Try to find your birth mother?

50. There is an election in your town next month. Your brother, who is too young to vote, decides to earn some money. He visits a candidate's office and pretends his mother sent him. He gets 10,000 yen a day to hand out flyers. After an hour he pretends he or his mother is sick and he goes home. The following days he goes to a different office. Every day he does the same thing. Is this right? Should he be stopped? What advice would you give? Is it wrong?

51. You work for a very small company. The boss's son is a good friend of yours. He asks you to clock in for him every morning; he is always late. If you don't do it, you will lose his friendship and you may get fired. What is the best way out of this dilemma?

52. Kemiko loves to help poor people. She works as a waitress in a busy restaurant. She always writes up two bills. One charges for coffee and tea which is supposed to be on the house (free). If the customers do not complain she and the cashier split the 'profits'. But Kemiko contributes all the extra money to dig wells in Africa. Is this OK? She is not stealing. She is just helping to develop fresh water in Africa?

53. Jill works in a fast in-and-out cleaners. Her brother is unemployed. Jill knows her customers well. So she lends her customers' shirts and suits to her brother to go for job interviews. She always has them ready when the customers come to pick them up. Is this OK? As long as the customers don't know, is it probably all right?
What do you think? What should she do? Doesn't she have an obligation to help her family?

54. Jack is a poor student who likes to put sugar in his tea. Once a week he goes to a coffee shop and secretly puts all the sugar he can into a plastic bag in his pocket. Is this OK? Is it stealing or do managers expect customers to steal sugar?

55.You and Bill work in the same company. Your wife and Bill's wife are good friends. Bill just got fired for taking the boss's daughter to a motel during work. He told his wife a different story. Should you tell your wife the truth? If Bill's wife finds out she will probably divorce him. What should you do?

56. Jon is a car salesperson. When he sells a car to old people he is supposed to lower the price $50.00 when he doesn't fill the gas tank. In fact he does not lower the price at all. (This increases his commission.) However, there is a good chance his deceit will be discovered. What should he do? What would you recommend?

57. Jack is a long distance truck driver. He has a wife in Seattle and a second one in Florida. He told you this one night when he was drunk. His wife is a classmate of yours from high school. Should you keep this a secret? Why? Why not?

58. You are friends with Tim and Tom Jones, identical twins. Tim is much smarter than Tom. You know that Tim took the SAT test twice so that both boys could go to the same university. If you tell someone no one will believe you, and you cannot prove your allegation. What should you do?

59. You work for a school district. You know that one teacher in the district forged his graduation certificate. He is an excellent teacher; parents and students appreciate him. If your boss finds out that you knew and did not tell him, he will fire you. What should you do?

60. Your best friend is getting married next month. He wants to have a large family. As you are a nurse at a clinic, you know his future wife cannot have children. Do you tell him? Are you obliged to tell/keep confidential secrets? If it were you what would do?

61. Your friend works in an expensive ski resort. He steals all the rich visitors' names and addresses. Later he will phone them to sell them securities or gold. Is this wrong? Does he have the right to copy addresses? Should you tell his employer?

62. You work for an insurance company. You know that your best friend's wife has been diagnosed with incurable cancer. Now your friend wants to increase the amount of life insurance he has on his wife. What would you recommend?

63. You and your friend argue about the best way to help the poor. He believes it is by donating money. You believe it is by not wasting food either at home or in restaurants. Which is the best way? Any ideas ?

64. In Japan, the death penalty is given for some murders. However, the convicted murderers do not know the date of their execution. Is this an additional punishment? Should they be given more notice?

65. You have just been selected to be minister of education. Your first official action would be to ……?

66. Your spouse has a very good friend of the opposite sex on the Internet. They never meet, but every week they spend hours talking to each other. Do you think this is OK?

67. Your teenage brother goes shopping for a handicapped neighbor. He buys cigarettes for both the handicapped person and himself. Your brother pays for his own cigarettes. Is this OK? Is it cheating?

68. You are a pharmacist. You found a way to sell generic medicine as brand name drugs. The profit is quite large but as your salary is low so you feel it is OK. The drugs are quite similar and patients think they are getting the more expensive one. Is it OK?

69. You have two friends who hate each other. Next week they are both having a party on the same day at the same time. You have been invited to both. What will you do?

70. Your sister is taking care of your grandmother who has Alzheimer's. You know she is spending grandma's money freely, and she may have gotten grandma to change her will. What are you going to do? Is it worth alienating your sister over money?

71. At a party you tried an illegal drug once. One boy who was at the party threatens to tell (your parents) the police if you don't give him $500.00. What will you do?

72. Your best friend has just been diagnosed with an incurable cancer. She wants you to help her commit suicide. What will you do?

73. You interview for a new job and get it. You need the excellent salary they are offering you, but you know the company is dishonest and cheats customers. You will....?

74. You are mountain climbing with two friends. You are all attached to the same rope. Both of them slip and you can save yourself by cutting the rope. They will fall off the mountain. Will you do it?

75. You drive up a mountain road and drive on an unpaved road into the forest. As night falls your car will not start and a thick fog covers the areas. What do you do?

76. You work for a very prestigious company. The boss's son or daughter likes you very much. He/she suggests you accompany him/her to a business meeting in Los Vegas. You think he/she has other 'business' in mind. What do you do?

77. The media is busy 'predicting' another earthquake and possible tsunami. What preparations have you made or are in the process of making? Where will you and your family meet in case everyone is not home during the crisis?

78. People who live alone are dying alone and sometimes found weeks after their deaths. What can we do to prevent this from happening? Whose fault is it - the family's or the city hall's?

79. If tomorrow we invent or discover a way to fuel cars with only water, how will the world change?

80. Would the mental ability to detect other people's negative or destructive thoughts be a boon to the world? What would change?

81. In Japan 30,000 people each year kill themselves. Do they have a right to do this? Should they be stopped? What can we do to decrease suicide?

82. Would you be in favor of a law making cigarette smoking illegal? Why/why not?

83. A new movement begins asking us to simplify our lives and become less materialistic. What are you willing to do to simplify your life?

84. People in America and Japan (to a much lesser degree) are becoming obese. Should the government mandate physical exercise for all non-handicapped citizens? Should fat people pay more for insurance and when riding on planes?

85. Drunk drivers kill many innocent people every year. What would be a suitable punishment for these drivers?

86. The state/country has set up a minimum wage. Is it OK for some unemployed people to voluntarily work for less than the minimum wage?

87. There is a lot of chewing gum on footpaths. Should the price of chewing gum be raised 5% to pay for workers to scrape it off roads and footpaths?

88. Should those with gardens be forced to grow their own vegetables?

89. Some sick old people have a bad quality of life. Would it be better to advise them to accept euthanasia? Would you help them to die peacefully?

90. Should the tax on cabarets and bars be raised to provide more money for unemployed parents with children or single parent homes?

91. Some countries have daylight saving time. Should it be introduced into your country too?

92. If predicting earthquakes becomes an exact science, would you leave your country to avoid a strong earthquake and tsunami?

93. Many countries are spending a lot of money on space exploration. Do you think this is a good idea or a waste of money? What are some of the benefits? What are some negative consequences?

94."Wasting one grain of rice shows disrespect to the farmers". Do people in in your country still feel this statement is true?

95. What is your favorite proverb? When does it mean? When do you use it?

96. Your brother has kidney problems. He needs a kidney. Would you be willing to give him one of yours?

97. The yoga teacher has a part time job selling cosmetics. She tries to sell them to her students. Is this wrong?

98. At a Japanese wedding the matchmaker reads out the educational history of the young couple. Is it wrong to lie and say one or both graduated from a university they never attended?

99. When you go for an interview for a job you can do well, is it OK to lie about your age?

100. If you were able to choose the illness or disease that kills you, which one would you pick?

101. Which is worse, to let a guilty person go unpunished or to imprison an innocent person? What are your reasons?

102. "The end justifies the means." (This means if our objective (aim) is good, then anything that helps us to achieve it is OK.) Do you agree?

103. In an ever changing world, would it be OK for Japan to have nuclear weapons just to protect the country?

104. Will education, science, knowledge, or religion solve all the world's problems?

105. What are the reasons for wars, conflicts, and terrorism? How can we avoid them?

106. If you, your spouse, your mother, and your child were in a sinking boat, which one would you save? (If you could save only one.) If you could save two?

107."Spare the rod and spoil the child"- do you agree with spanking? Recall your own experience and your child rearing techniques.

108. Does one lie make one a liar? Are there 'good lies'?

109. Should murderers be put to death by the state? (Capital punishment.) If they killed a member of your family would you feel the same way?

110. Does winning a lot of money (lottery) bring happiness?

111. Some people are martyrs for a cause. Is there any cause you would be willing to die for?

112. If you had only a short time to live, how would you spend that time?

113. You go to the recycle shop to buy a coin purse. You find an old one with a secret pocket in it with a gold coin. Do you just buy it quietly or do you tell the store owner?

114. Everyone in your class is teasing an unpopular overweight student with a bad attitude. Would you be willing to befriend that student? How would you stop the teasing? (Teen topic)

115. The Internet, the latest phones, and social networking sites allow us to communicate with more people worldwide. Is this real communication? Do we interact enough with our neighbors? What is real communication?

116. Now we have surveillance cameras everywhere in public. They prevent crime by spying on people. Do you think this is a good idea or are you happy with them?

117. Genetic engineering has made great progress recently. We are now able to have 'designer' babies. We can choose the height, weight, eye color, and even the IQ. If you had enough money would you prefer to have a 'designer' baby? Why/why not?

118. You have been picked for a jury in a murder trial. Would it be easy /difficult/impossible for you to recommend the death penalty for someone who is found guilty of murder?

119. Some insurance companies charge smokers more for insurance than non-smokers. Is this fair? How about people who eat junk food and don't exercise?

120. If you were married and could not have children would you adopt a child? Why/why not? Would you adopt a girl or boy?

121. You live in a nice neighborhood. A friendly young family wishes to buy a house on your street. Should you tell them that someone was murdered in that house?

122. Would you be willing to pay higher taxes so that your city can host the Olympics?

123. Should cars be banned from city centers? What would some of the results be?

124. If your spouse disappeared how long would you wait before getting married again?

125. Will the Internet put newspapers out of business? Where do you get your news? Do you think the media is fair and balanced?

126. A lot of money is spent to make sure some animal species does not become extinct. Is this a good idea? Why/why not?

127. Bhutan is a country with GNH – gross national happiness. Are the people in your country happy? Why/why not? What is the best way to be happy?

128. "The punishment should fit the crime". What would be a suitable punishment for pick pocketing, stealing, lying under oath, cheating on a test, etc.

129. Do we learn anything from children's stories? Which one is your favorite? What lesson does it teach?

130. Do you agree with the following statement by Dale Carnegie:" Success is getting what you want; happiness is wanting what you get."

131. "Students should get their first cell phones when they are …… ". Give reasons for your opinion and be able to politely disagree with other opinions.

132. You and your spouse-to-be want to have a simple wedding. You want to donate the money saved to an orphanage or save it for your life together. Your parents are adamant that you have a big wedding. What will you do? Can you work out a compromise?

133. You have been asked to get rid of one national holiday. Which one would you eliminate? Why?

134. If asked to add a holiday to the calendar what month would you insert it in? What kind of holiday would you decide on? Why?

135. Some swimming pools make people cover tattoos when swimming. Is this discrimination? Should they be allowed?

136. We as a society seem to be getting more violent now. Are video games part of the problem? Or are parents unable to raise their children correctly? What steps should we take to improve our lives?

137. You are dating a wonderful person whom you intend to marry. How much of your past are you willing to share with him/her? Should you keep some things secret?

138. The paparazzi follow celebrities around and invade their privacy. Should laws protect famous stars/athletes from these intrusive photographers or are they just nosy journalists?

139. Imagine you are at a Wedding Fair for singles. What questions do you ask a possible mate? How do you answer questions about your values?

140. Your company has asked you to come up with ways to make weddings less expensive. What are some ideas you would mention?

142. You have to give the eulogy at your friend's funeral. What would you say?

143. Your daughter/son wants to get a tattoo, cosmetic surgery, and Botox injections. What would you tell her/him?

144. When you make a new friend what qualities do you look for? Honesty? Sense of humor? Same age? Things in common? Same social status? Same religion? Same education? Etc.

145. What do you remember most about the 20th century? What will you tell your grandchildren?

146. Would the world better off if we had only one language? What would be some of the advantages disadvantages? Esperanto?

147. Will electronic books replace paper books in a few more years? Why or why not?

148. Will robots and inter active computers replace teachers?

149. Would you like to live to be 150 or 200 years old? Why/why not?

150. In Japanese high school baseball, pitchers have to pitch almost every day. Is this damaging to their arms? Is it a form of child abuse?

151. Do you agree that professional athletes' salaries are too high? Give reasons for your opinion.

152. Cram schools: necessary or unnecessary?

***

In Other Words:

'In Other Words' is an effort to help students improve their vocabulary. Each article is written twice with the second one containing more difficult words. These articles of different lengths could be used as discussion topics. The content varies from experience to commentary and opinion. As well as introducing new vocabulary, they aim to stimulate thought, interest, and conversation. They are not in any special order and they are not uniform in length. The narratives and expository articles focus on simple topics that many students can relate to. I hope you find some that you like. Enjoy.

1. Friendship:

I got to know Kenji Suzuki while I was in college. He was the only non-American student in my class. We shared a room in the dormitory with two other students. He and I became friends even though we were both shy. We studied together and it was helpful to both of us. I helped him with his English and he helped me with math - my weakest subject. After graduation we just exchanged Christmas cards as we both were busy working.

Last year I had a chance to visit Japan on business. My boss let me add a few days' vacation, so I wrote to Kenji. I had no idea he knew so much about the history of Kyoto. I was treated like a king. He took me all over the old city. He knew everything about the old temples, castles, and gardens.

We even went to one castle corridor where the floor boards still creak loudly if walked on. It was built to prevent sneak attacks on the castle. No one knows how the carpenters did this.

He explained the history of Buddhism, Shinto, and militarism. He got me to try tasty Japanese food. I now know the difference between good and not so good sushi. I came home with recipes for Japanese tempura and curry rice. He even took me to a Japanese public bath where we all washed together and soaked in a very hot bath about half the size of a swimming pool. I don't know how to thank him. If he comes to see me in America I hope I can repay his kindness.

2.Friendship:

When I was an undergraduate at the university, I made the acquaintance of Kenji Suzuki. He was one of only a few foreign undergraduates in our university. We roomed together in a college dormitory with two other freshmen.

We were both not so outgoing so we hit it off well. We studied together as it was mutually beneficial. I tutored him in English and his expertise in mathematics really helped me. Math is my educational nemesis. After graduation we went our respective ways but kept in touch through Christmas cards.

Then last year my company provided with me with an opportunity to visit Japan. My CEO even allowed me to combine business with pleasure by including a few days' vacation in Japan. I contacted Kenji immediately.

He treated me like royalty. (a VIP). He was my tour guide and escort all through Kyoto. He was a virtual encyclopedia of history and a gold mine of information about the ancient buildings and gardens of Kyoto. Kenji provided the background history of each temple, shrine, castle, and garden. We even visited Gojo Castle where the sensitive corridor floor boards make it impossible for anyone to sneak in quietly. Even now, no one can figure out how the carpenters accomplished this remarkable feat.

 Kenji shared his extensive knowledge of Buddhism, Shinto, and militarism to make my sightseeing so much more interesting and memorable.

He even got me to indulge in some typical Japanese food. Now I can discriminate between good and average sushi. I am now the proud owner of uncommon recipes for tempura and Japanese curry rice. Experiencing the Japanese public bath was another unforgettable experience. Everyone washed outside the bath and then soaked in a bath almost the size of a small swimming pool. It was most refreshing. I owe Kenji a debt of gratitude, and I hope he visits America again so I can reciprocate his kindness.

3.Boston:

If you ever get a chance you should visit the city of Boston. It is one of the oldest cities in America and has a lot of history. It was in Boston where the fight for freedom began. The people there showed great cleverness and courage in fighting against the powerful forces of England. In the beginning they looked weak but they never gave in. They believed in each other and in their aim. These qualities led them to victory as they lit the torch of American independence.

Today Boston is a great center of learning. It is home to some of the best universities and colleges in the world. A degree from such a school opens doors and prepares graduates to be productive citizens of the world.

In the world of medicine, Boston has many famous hospitals and research centers. It is on the cutting edge of new medical technologies that will help us live longer and healthier. So Boston is proud of its past and present- a city that influences and benefits all of America, and indeed, all of the world.

4.Boston:

 If at all possible, avail of the opportunity to visit the historical city of Boston. As well as being relatively old, it is the cradle of the American Revolution. The patriots there demonstrated great ingenuity and bravery in combating and resisting the power of the British Empire. As the war commenced, the Bostonians chances of success looked slim, but improved with perseverance. Their mutual trust in each other and in the validity of their cause led them to victory. They fanned the spark of revolution into a great flame of independence.

Today Boston is an educational metropolis boasting of such fine educational facilities as Harvard and M.I.T. Graduates of Boston universities are often cosmopolitan contributors to fields that improve the lives of everyone on this planet.

 In the field of medicine, the city is without equal. Research centers and hospitals attached to universities develop cutting edge technologies that benefit everyone. It is no exaggeration to say that America, and indeed the world, owes a debt of gratitude to the great city of Boston.

5. Grandpa:

Before my grandfather got very old he lost his hearing. It was hard to speak to him. We had to shout to get through to him. So we often pretended not to notice him and left him out of our conversations. We openly talked about him and joked about what we would do with his money when he died. He smiled and tried to go along with our mean way of treating him.

 But although he was deaf he was far from being stupid. Without telling anyone, he went out and got hearing aids. He had them for two months before anyone noticed. During that time he changed his will at least two times.

My grandfather is now in his second childhood. He says the same thing over and over again, and does not even remember saying it once. He is always looking for his glasses. Sometimes he "finds" them on his head.

He remembers his early years much better than what happened last night. It is sad to see his mind waste away while his body loses strength. Is this what we have to look forward to while waiting to see who Grandpa left in or out of his will.

6. Grandpa:

My grandfather's first sign of advancing age was hearing loss. Meaningful communication with him was almost impossible. It included shouting, writing, and gesturing. Gradually we just ignored him and left him marinate in silence. It went so far as discussing him in his presence as he was stone deaf. We even discussed how we would spend the inheritance he would leave us after his demise. Grandpa just smiled and accepted our rude way of acting.

But deafness does not mean stupidity. Unknown to us, he acquired hearing aids. It was two months before anyone even realized this, and of course Grandpa did not mention it at all. During that time he changed the provisions of his will at least twice.

Now my grandfather is senile. His constant repetition of the same sentences tends to be tedious. Sometimes his forgetfulness leads him to search for his glasses when they are located on his head!

His long term memory is excellent as he proves by recounting his early years in minute detail. His short term memory is fading fast. It is sobering to realize that all of us are destined for the same fate. So while we contemplate our own physical and mental deterioration, we have to wonder how Grandpa's last will and testament will contribute to contentment or contention in the family.

7. Tenant Rules:

The manager of the apartment which I rented told me some of the rules. Namely, if there is a big problem in the apartment, then the owner or someone sent by him, can go in without my OK, or even if I am not there. Parents always have to take care of and control their children. If the children break anything, the parents have to pay for it. Tenants should keep the laundry room tidy. Washed clothes should not be left in the washing machines as others may want to use the machines.

Renters can store some of their things in the storage area which has their apartment number on it. No renter can keep gas, or other dangerous stuff in his/her apartment, garage, or storage area.

Car parking is limited. Each apartment is given one parking space. The parking structure is four stories high and cars are stacked one on top of another using an elevator type system. Parking or getting one's car to or from the top of the parking structure takes time. If someone else is getting a car it doubles your wait time. As a result, parking spaces on the ground level are most attractive.

If someone leaves the apartment complex, a lottery will be held if that tenant had a ground floor parking space.

Families with two cars should find other parking nearby which can cost between five or ten thousand yen a month. Car owners may not repair cars or do oil changes in parking spaces. For other questions not covered in this paper, please talk to the apartment manager.

8. Tenant Rules:

The following regulations are an integral part of the renter's agreed upon contract. In the event of an emergency, or if there is a good reason to believe one exists, management reserves the right to enter the premises during the tenant's absence without prior permission. At all times, children must be under the supervision of their parents or guardians. Parents will be financially responsible for any damage caused by their children or guests. Each tenant is responsible for maintaining a neat and clean laundry facility. Washed clothes must be removed from washing machines promptly so that other tenants can avail of the machines.

Personal belongings may be stored only in designated storage areas. Gasoline, flammable liquids, or other combustibles may not be stored in the apartment, carport, or storage area. Parking is assigned and limited to one space per tenant. The parking tower is where most of the cars will park. The structure is four stories high and drivers should be aware that parking or retrieving cars takes time. If two cars are being retrieved at the same time, the time needed is double. Consequently, a limited number of parking spaces on the ground level are in demand. If one becomes vacant a lottery will be held. Tenants with two cars will have to find alternate parking nearby. The cost ranges from five to ten thousand yen per month. Tenants are not allowed to change the oil or repair their cars in parking spaces. For other concerns not enumerated in this document, please consult the onsite apartment manager.

9. Smoke:

We have a beautiful apartment, near stores and near the station. But there is one thing I don't like about it. The people next door to us smoke a lot. When they are outside smoking, they share the smoke with us. Neither my wife nor I smoke. We hate smoke. We bought a little fan and it blows the smoke back to them. Maybe they will stop or move!

My wife and I discussed ways to let them know we dislike smoke, but we do not want to start a war with our neighbors. It is better to keep the peace so that we can live stress free.

We do not have a mutual friend or go-between who could help solve this dilemma. Of course the ones causing the trouble are unaware of our problem so we decided to just keep quiet and put up with it.

10. Smoke

We purchased a beautiful apartment that is quite convenient. It is adjacent to a shopping center, and within walking distance of the train station. However, it has one major disadvantage – the neighbors are chain smokers. When they smoke on their veranda, we get the 'benefit' of their second-hand smoke. Neither my wife nor I indulge in this bad habit. In fact we detest smoke. We purchased a fan which we placed strategically on our veranda. The smoke is wafted back to where it came from. Maybe they will get the idea and quit smoking or move to another residence!

My wife and I considered direct confrontation but this might only exacerbate matters. Prudence is the better part of valor in order to live in peace. A mutual friend would be invaluable in this situation but we have no one available. The ones causing the problem are oblivious to our feelings, so we have opted to suffer in silence.

11. Home Stay:

Momoka just came back from a six-week home stay in America. She learned a lot there and noticed everything. On the phone she told me a few things that she found unusual. First, she saw many fat people. Some were so fat they could hardly fit into chairs in a restaurant. Of course, she feels restaurants are part of the problem. They give very big helpings, and then after dinner many diners even eat a rich sweet dessert. Even Momoka put on a few pounds herself.

Another interesting thing was the weekend yard sales. People just put all the things they do not want on the lawn, and sell them to their neighbors. She said it was a great way to buy books and comics. They even sell furniture, beds, and household appliances. Prices are not so high so there is a lot of buying and selling. It benefits both sellers and buyers. However, she doubts that most Japanese would have the courage to do that in Japan.

12. Homestay:

Momoka has just returned from her home stay in America. Nothing escaped her observant eyes. She was especially surprised at seeing so many over-weight and obese people. Some found it hard to squeeze into chairs at a restaurant. She blames restaurants for making the portions so huge.

Of course ordering rich, sugary desserts does not help waist lines either. Maybe even Momoka gave in to temptation; she herself gained weight while there.

Another interesting phenomenon she noticed was the weekend garage sales Americans have no qualms about trying to sell their junk to their neighbors. Excess items are offered for sale at bargain price. So it's a win-win situation for both buyer and seller.   -175-

The seller gets rid of useless items while the buyer is happy to pick up 'treasures' for a pittance. So it is a win-win situation for both seller and buyer. Even Momoka availed of these opportunities to pick up some books at bargain prices. However, she feels that Japanese people would be too embarrassed to initiate yard sales here.

13.Funeral Etiquette:

My friend's father died last week. So I do not know what to do. He was a Christian so maybe they do things differently. I think I should send flowers and a card. I do want to say I am sad to hear of his death. In Japan we always give money. Is there anyone we can ask for help? I don't want to do anything that will add to their sorrow. Is there anyone we can ask for advice?

14. Funeral Etiquette:

I just read the obituary of my friend's father in the newspaper. I am not sure what the proper etiquette (procedure) is.
As he was Christian maybe they have different funeral rituals. Perhaps I should send a card offering my condolences, and have some flowers delivered to their home. Offering money at a time like this might be considered gauche (impolite/rude). Can we pick someone's brain and discover what is expected and acceptable?

15. A Mother's View on Education

Thanks for helping me to move last week. Also, thanks for the present. I did not want to take it, but your mother made me. The necklace is made of real pearls. I think Mr. Mikimoto himself made it. I really should not have such expensive jewelry. Finishing college is not such a big deal anymore. However, your mother always pushes people to learn more, and dislikes students who drop out. That is why you are like a GPS- three degrees from Harvard!

Your parents' ideas on education are unusual. They encouraged you and all your brothers and sisters to have at least four years of college. They wanted all of you to learn to think logically, be able to do research, live independently, and become good time managers, all of which are the foundation of education.

So choosing a university that allows students to grow without being brainwashed is the first step.

Many colleges churn out graduates who just echo the ideas of their teachers. They seem to have forgotten how to logically discuss ideas. Your mother is proud to say that half of the family is liberal and the other half is not. It is very exciting to go to a home where the TV is off and intellectual discussion rages. We need more homes like yours.

16. A Mother's View on Education:

I wish to express my gratitude for your recent assistance when I was moving. Also, I really appreciate the exquisite gift. I did not want to accept it but your mother insisted. The necklace is made of genuine Japanese pearls. I suspect it was assembled by Mr. Mikimoto himself. I don't deserve such a wonderful gift. Graduating from university is not such a superb achievement any more. You mother always encourages people to get as much education as possible. She resents students who quit before graduation. Maybe that is why you got so much education. You are like a GPS – three degrees from Harvard!

Your parents espouse rather progressive ideas about education. They made sure that you and all your siblings got at least a B.A. from a four-year university. They required that each one of you could engage in dialectical discussions, conduct individual research, and live independently as efficient time managers. These are the basic pillars of education.

So choosing a university that promotes diversity of thought was the first requirement. Many universities churn out brainwashed graduates who can only echo their professors' opinions. They eschew discussions and intellectual confrontation.

Meanwhile your mother boasts that half of your family is liberal and the other half is conservative. It is always refreshing and educational to visit a home where stimulating discussions keep the TV off.

17. Strange Homework:

The teacher gave us very strange homework. We had to stop people in the street and get their opinions about government, food, wages, health, and what they believe in. Even though we never asked people for their names or addresses, most people kept away from us. Perhaps with so much crime in society, people do feel like talking to strangers. Perhaps if I had a big sign asking for help with my homework, more people would have felt sorry for me.

I am afraid to tell my teacher about my experience as it may give her an idea for our next homework. It could possibly be asking us to find out why people do not like surveys. A few passers-by were very helpful when we told them it was homework. My classmate Jack talked to the most people. He gave a balloon to women with small children, so they felt they had to stop and talk. Next time I will try that.

18. Strange Homework:

Our professor gave us rather unique homework. We had to interview people on the street and tabulate their responses. The survey questions dealt with politics, diet, salaries, health, and religion. Even though respondents could remain anonymous, most people tended to ignore us as they rushed past. The ever-increasing crime rate in our cities makes people wary of strangers. Perhaps a blatant sign soliciting help with homework would have proved effective.

However, apprising our teacher of our difficulties might inspire her to make this complaint the topic of our next assignment. A few people were very considerate when they learned it was homework. A classmate called Jack interviewed the most people by far. He presented a balloon to mothers with infants. Then they felt obliged to talk to him. Next time, I will try his successful technique.

19. The Elderly:

In Japan, there are many elderly people. The Japanese seem to live longer than people in other countries. Usually the women live about five years longer than the men. Some writers feel that the good Japanese food has a lot to do with this.

People eat a lot of fish, vegetables, and fruit. Japanese rice does not have any dangerous poisons in it, and can be eaten daily.

Meat is eaten but in smaller amounts than in Western countries. The meat is from cattle that graze unlike the corn fed beef many Americans are used to. The regular diet includes a variety of beans, sometimes fermented, as well as seaweed. Green tea is much more popular than coffee. It even makes up for the harm done by smoking. Also, the people walk much more than those living in other developed countries.

 Housewives go shopping almost daily to buy the freshest fruit and vegetables. Most of the work force uses trains or buses to get to work. So that means they have a lot of walking to do. However, long life has a down side to it. Senior citizens often live alone without much money. Some get sick and die without ever seeing a doctor. Others feel lonely and useless, so they kill themselves. One of the odd things about Japan is so many people and so much loneliness.

20. The Elderly:

The percentage of elderly people in Japan is increasing rapidly. Japanese life expectancy tends to be the longest in the world, with women outliving men by an average of five years. Age researchers, called gerontologists, credit the healthy Japanese diet for this longevity.

Consumption of fish, vegetables, fruit, beans, and seaweed is more beneficial than the American diet. Japanese rice has almost no toxins in it and can be eaten daily.

 Beef is usually from grass fed cattle and is much healthier than the corn fed variety common in the U.S. Green tea seems to act as an antidote to tobacco use, and may compensate for or negate the bad effects of smoking. Another factor is that walking is much more common in Japan than in other developed countries.

Housewives walk to the local neighborhood store to purchase fresh food daily. Most workers commute to work using public transportation and this ensures a lot of walking. However, long life has a negative dimension; namely, many elderly are forced to live alone on a very limited income. Often their health deteriorates and many die prematurely due to lack of medical attention. Others find the solitude depressing and commit suicide. One of the contradictions of Japan is so many people but so much loneliness.

21. Population:

The number of people in Japan is getting smaller. There are many reasons for this. Women want to get a college education and go to work. Then they can enjoy their lives, have new hobbies, and enjoy travel. As a result, they get married when they are older, and some do not get married at all. Men seem to work long hours and are not home to help with raising children. Many young women feel this in unfair.

Another problem is finding wives for men living in country areas. As young women rush to work in big cities, young farmers find it difficult to find a wife willing to forgo the city. Some villages and country areas hold 'wedding fairs' so young men and women can get a chance to meet with a view to marriage. Some farmers even get wives from other Asian countries. The government is trying to help by giving money to couples who have children. It is anyone's guess how this problem will be finally solved.

22. Population:

The population of Japan is decreasing steadily. Many possible reasons for this phenomenon are being discussed. One possible reason is that women now prefer to get as much education as possible and seek gainful employment.

Thus, they can pursue interesting careers, engage in exciting hobbies, and afford trips overseas. Consequently, they tend to postpone marriage and some even avoid it completely. Men on the other hand tend to "marry" their companies, and overtime prevents them from cooperating in the raising of children. Modern women naturally feel this is not a recipe for a happy home life.

Young men engaged in agriculture face great challenges in finding a bride. Most young ladies abandon their rural surroundings as they become attracted to life in large urban areas. Even though some communities host "wedding fairs" with a view to facilitating matrimonial bliss, some farmers despair of finding a spouse in Japan, so they marry brides from other Asian countries. The government has a stake in this too and provides financial incentives to couples who have children. How this problem will ultimately be resolved is presently a matter of conjecture.

23. An Accident:

In the town of Kemendo there was a big accident two Saturdays ago. A large van driven by a teenager hit a mini car driven by a mother with two small infants. The driver of the van was not hurt but those in the mini car were taken to hospital. They will have to stay there for at least three months.

Police said the cause of the accident was the van trying to pass a slow moving car on a curve. Police are trying to find out if the driver of the van had been drinking. In Japan drunk driving is a major crime and is punished severely, usually it includes a long time in prison and a big fine. If the driver is found guilty, there will be one less careless driver to worry about for a long time.

24 .An Accident:

The town of Kemendo was the scene of a horrific accident the Saturday before last. An SUV driven by a 19-year-old driver crashed into a mini car driven by a mother with two small children. The teenage driver was not seriously injured but the occupants of the mini car were transported to a local hospital.

Their condition was listed as serious though not life-threatening. A hospital spokesman intimated that their hospitalization will last for at least three months.

Police believe the accident was caused by the van trying to overtake a slow moving car at a curve on a two-lane highway. Police are now investigating whether there was alcohol involved. In Japan punishment for drunk driving is severe, and usually involves lengthy incarceration along with a substantial fine. If it is ascertained that alcohol was involved, Japan will have one less reckless drive to worry about for quite a long time.

25 . English:

As the number of English speakers increase, the spoken word changes. There are many grammar mistakes made in everyday conversation, and usually people act as if they never happened. Many people wonder if this is a good or bad thing. As an English speaker, I feel that a variety of English is a good thing. It shows the language is alive and changing. Often mistakes, if made continually, tend to become accepted.

For example: "I don't think it will rain' is not considered wrong, although some would prefer to hear: 'I think it will not rain'. We often say 'I bet it won't rain.' But you will never hear 'I don't bet it will rain.' 'Can' now often replaces the more polite 'may. 'Can I borrow your pen' instead of 'may I borrow your pen'.

Words change through usage, and often the meaning changes 100%. For example, the word 'homely' in the U.S. means 'ugly'. At first glance, it looks like it should have something to do with 'home'. It is not known how it came to mean ugly; perhaps it was used as a joke meaning the opposite of what was said.

'Manufacture' is a pure Latin word originally meaning 'made by hand'. Now it only means 'made by machine in a factory'. 'Awful' has a few different meanings. Usually it means' very great' or 'very terrible', and its original meaning of 'causing awe' is forgotten.

Some words found their way into English by being borrowed from other languages. 'Tsunami' has been taken directly from Japanese to describe a powerful tidal wave. 'Sukosh' is another Japanese word that is gaining popularity. In Japanese it means 'a little' or 'a few'. 'Galore' means 'a lot' or 'many' taken from Gaelic (Irish). We can also thank the Irish for 'smithereens' which means 'little pieces'.

Sometimes the first letters of words used to describe an item become a new word. 'Scuba' is a well-known example. S.C.U.B.A. means 'self-contained underwater breathing apparatus'. 'Radar' originally meant an instrument used for 'radio detecting and ranging'. A young urban professional became a 'yuppie' using the first letters of each word, and then changing the ending to rhyme with 'hippie'. 'Cop' coming from C.O.P. (constable of police) is now a word used for a police officer. Checking the history and meaning of words can be an interesting hobby.

26. English:

As the number of English speakers increase, this inevitably leads to variations in the language. However, solecisms and grammar mistakes are usually ignored in everyday conversation. Linguists and language purists do not always agree on whether this is acceptable progress or not. As an English speaker, I feel that this shows the vitality of language. (Latin does not change so we call it a 'dead language'.)

Over time, mistakes in grammar become accepted, and gradually they find their way into print. The following examples will clarify this. 'I don't think it will rain' is considered as correct as 'I think it will not rain'. Language purists might prefer the latter sentence. When analyzed strictly, 'I don't think' sounds rather strange, but we have gotten accustomed to hearing it. However, 'I bet it won't rain' cannot be replaced with 'I don't bet it will rain.' Another acceptable usage is 'can' for the more polite 'may'.

Through usage, some words change 100% and become the opposite of their original meaning. How did 'homely' come to mean 'ugly'? Perhaps it was used sarcastically or humorously to mean the opposite of something you would not find at home?

The word 'manufacture' from Latin, literally means 'made by hand'. Two hundred years later it means an item made by machine in a factory. 'Awful' now means 'terrible' or 'very great'. Its original meaning of 'inspiring awe' is usually forgotten.

Borrowing words from other languages also demonstrates vitality. 'Tsunami' meaning a 'tidal wave', and 'sukosh' meaning 'little' or 'few', have come from Japanese.

Both words are popular, but the former is probably more common than the latter, thanks to the March 11, 2011, disaster in northeastern Japan. 'Galore' and 'smithereens' meaning 'a lot of' and 'little broken pieces' respectively, have come to English from Irish (Gaelic).

Acronyms have developed into independent words with the original meaning likely to be forgotten. 'Scuba' is a well-known water sport with the word standing for: 'self-contained underwater breathing apparatus'. 'Radio detecting and ranging' was shortened to 'radar'; 'constable of police' became 'cop'; 'yuppie' came from combining the initials for 'young urban professional 'and rhyming it with 'hippie'. Etymology can be a fascinating and interesting study for everyone.

27. Puns:

A pun is said to be a play on words that sound the same, or using one word that can have a double meaning. In Japanese, there are many words that sound the same, so we find many examples of puns in the culture. The word for frog sounds like the word for return. So many Japanese have a tiny porcelain or plastic frog in their purses or hand bags so that their money will return to them.

The Japanese word for sea bream is similar to the word for celebration. So naturally sea bream is eaten at important parties. The Japanese for five yen can sound like the words for good relationships. As a result, five yen coins are often on key chains. When visiting a shrine at New Year's, people give five, fifty, or 500 yen to make sure good luck follows them throughout the year.

But punning is not always good. The word for four can also mean death, so it is not a very popular number. Some hospitals and hotels do not use the number four at all. Maybe that is another reason why Japanese people live longer than most.

28. Puns:

A pun is defined as a play on words that have a similar pronunciation, or it can be one word that can have two meanings. Japanese culture takes punning to a new dimension as many words sound the same although they are written differently. 'Kaeru' is the word for frog and also the word for 'return'. Consequently, many Japanese make sure they insert a miniature porcelain or plastic frog in their purses or handbags. It is supposed to ensure that their money will return to them.

'Tai' is the Japanese word for 'sea bream' as well as being half of the word 'medetai' which means 'happy celebration'. Naturally, sea bream is eaten at many lavish celebrations and parties. 'Go en' can mean 'five yen' or 'good relationships'. Five-yen coins are often attached to key chains and even to gifts to bring about success in relationships. When visiting a shrine or temple at New Year's, contributions of five, fifty, or five hundred yen are supposed to provide good luck for the contributor throughout the year.

However, there are also some unlucky puns. 'Shi' the word for 'four' can also mean 'death'. As a result, some hospitals and hotels have eliminated four as a room number. Another reason for Japanese longevity?

29. Tipping:

In most countries tipping is an added cost to eating, traveling, or getting good service. Long ago T.I.P. just stood for "To insure promptness or promptitude." It was given only to servants, and many salaried workers were insulted if they were given tips. Little by little this changed, and now it is thought to be part of many workers' salaries.

It seems that in the U.S. many employers pay very low wages to restaurant staff, sometimes even less than the minimum wage set by the government or state. Diners are supposed to pay between 15 and 20% of their bill to make sure wait staff get a living wage. So what was first called a 'gratuity', namely, something of value that one gives freely, is now forced and taken for granted.

To make sure it is not forgotten, it is very often added to the bill. Most countries have some kind of tipping system. The only difference is that in some places it is supposed to be done quietly and secretly. Fortunately for travelers, a few countries do not have tipping at all. Japan and Australia are two that provide service without charging for it. But do not expect tipping to end any time soon.

30. Tipping:

All over the world, diners and travelers have to factor in the cost of tipping if they wish to enjoy good service. Originally, the acronym just stood for "To Improve Promptitude or Promptness". (Now it could mean "to increase pay".) Salaried employees used to be insulted if offered a tip. Nowadays employers consider tips as part of salary, and consequently offer workers a low salary, sometimes even below the mandated minimum wage.

 Diners are expected to pay 15 or 20 % of their bill to make sure wait staff are adequately compensated. So what was originally thought to be a gratuity, something given freely– is compulsory and demanded. Some establishments even add it to a bill as a service charge so it cannot be avoided.

Most countries have some kind of tipping system. The only difference is that in some places it is expected to be done more discreetly. Fortunately, Japan and Australia provide service without expecting or even accepting tips. But if you expect tipping to disappear, don't hold your breath.

31. Older Workers:

In Japan, age is a very important topic and most Japanese want to know the age of their neighbors. When applying for a job, age is usually on the first or second line of the application. (It makes it easier for the HR department to know how to rate the applicant.) As the population of Japan grays, and as the economy gets better, companies might do well to think about older workers. Older workers have a lot to offer and it is not very difficult to list the advantages they bring to employers.

First is knowledge. They know how companies work and they are able to adjust to different personalities much better than recent graduates. They are likely to be experts in at least one field of business and can improve on the insights more recent employees. Their experience of 40 years enables them to avoid the pitfalls of the inexperienced who know so much unproved theory.

Another thing in favor of hiring the elderly is that they tend to be permanent. Younger workers are often ready to move to companies that offer them more salary, and their company loyalty is suspect. Having older workers removes the necessity of having to keep training new young workers.

Childcare is usually not a problem for older workers. So when hired they do not worry about cram school costs or college fees. They are usually satisfied with their salaries and are thankful to have a place to work. Being in time for work is a given and they work hard even without much supervision. The only possible down side to hiring older worker is that their health insurance may be costly, but they can stay covered under national health insurance and even this does not become a problem. So can we expect Japanese companies to change and worry more about a worker's experience than his/her date of birth? Only time will tell.

32. Older Workers:

An almost morbid curiosity about the age of neighbors and acquaintances seems to be an integral part of Japanese culture. Even job applications are structured to reveal the age of applicants on the first line. This makes it easier and faster for the HR department to find the youngest applicant. As the number of elderly workers increase and as the economy recovers, companies could do worse than reconsider the value of graying employees. It is not difficult to mention the advantages pursuant to hiring workers who are considered 'over the hill'.

The first benefit is knowledge. Older workers know the inner workings of corporate entities and they have honed their interpersonal skills in the workplace. Compared to recent university graduates, elderly workers are more likely to be experts in one or two aspects of business, and they can complement the ideas of younger inexperienced staff. Experience of 40 plus years enables them to avoid the pitfalls of younger workers who give too much credibility to theoretical solutions.

Another benefit in hiring older people is that they tend to be permanent. Younger workers, especially nowadays, are often like migratory birds just waiting for the appropriate season to depart. Hiring and training newcomers, whose loyalty is equally suspect, can prove costly to employers.

Care for children is never a problem for those nearing retirement. Educational expenses are usually a thing of the past and most are extremely grateful to be gainfully employed. They are punctual and capable of working independently without supervision. Even worries about higher health insurance can be avoided if these senior citizens maintain their national insurance coverage.

So optimistically, when can we expect Japanese companies to mine the gold that is an older experienced work force? Probably when necessity forces them to admit the obvious.

33. Matchmaking:

Long before the invention of the Internet, people used to have special men or women to broker marriage. These matchmakers helped shy or remote singles to become couples. As cities grew, the sense of community got lost, so now we have a technological matchmaker – an Internet website, or to be exact, over 1500 websites. Their dual function is to increase marital bliss and make a profit.

According to statistics, they gross close to one billion dollars every year and help thousands to find true love and marriage. The websites have to tread a fine line by being successful, profitable, and competitive, while avoiding being just a front for sexual trysts. Usually the more expensive the site the more trustworthy it is. Some claim to use scientific methods to pair up couples. This usually means using extensive questionnaires to find out likes and dislikes.

Applicants can mention values, religion, interests, education, and hobbies that they find acceptable. Some demand partners from a specific ethnic group and with a certain body size. Distance and anonymity allow for these demands to be addressed. The potential couple can communicate without giving their names or addresses until they feel comfortable with each other. A meeting can then be arranged so Cupid can do his thing.

Urban sprawl and long commutes often prevent singles from meeting other marriageable singles, so the Internet matchmakers are necessary. The pool of potential brides and grooms is not limited to one region, as it now can include the whole world.

Couples who have found happiness through matchmaking websites are loud in their praise, while the still unmatched are less enthusiastic.

I am sure it will only be a matter of time when a wedding ceremony will have a robot holding a computer acting as best man.

34. Matchmaking:

In the not so distant past, in rural communities, young people interested in being married were introduced to each other by matchmakers. These facilitators were especially appreciated by reserved or remote singles, whose dream of nuptial bliss depended on them for fulfillment. Urbanization sounded the death knell of community, so a technological matchmaker materialized on the Internet to fill the vacuum. What began as one website soon increased exponentially to more than 1500. Their dual purpose is to promote marital happiness while making a handsome profit for the companies involved.

Thousands of satisfied and some dissatisfied customers have parted with close to a billion dollars proving that money can buy love. With so much competition, the websites have to show they are successful, profitable, and trustworthy. A few are nothing more than sites offering sex for sale. Usually the more expensive sites are trustworthy, but caveat emptor. The more reputable websites employ extensive questionnaires which provide as much background information as six months' exclusive dating.

Singles can mention their core values, religion, personal likes and dislikes, as well as their hobbies and education. Some include the desired dimensions and ethnicity of their future spouse. In the initial stage of their communication, distance and anonymity make this possible.

If friendly communication continues or intensifies, a meeting can be arranged, and names and locations may be divulged. Then it is up to Cupid's arrows.

Are Internet matchmaking sites really necessary? The answer would have to be a definite yes. Large urban areas force young people to commute long distances thus preventing them from meeting other marriageable singles.
The Internet websites troll the whole world to find hundreds of young people hoping for a ringing conclusion to their bachelorhood. Successfully matched couples tend to exaggerate the worth of these websites; the unmatched are predictably less enthusiastic.

Technology is here to stay. So I am looking forward to attending a wedding in which the best man is a robot holding a computer -- displaying the appropriate matchmaking website of course.

35. Gambling:

A."I bet you can't give up gambling". B. "I bet I can". A. "Sorry, you lose."
Gambling probably dates back to when our cavemen ancestors competed in games of stone-throwing at some mobile or immobile targets. The desire to get something for nothing, or something for very little effort, is part of being human. Even educated people, who supposedly know mathematics, like to risk money on the results of activities that they cannot control. Remembering a good feeling and trying to recapture it lets gamblers forget that they are really grasping at shadows.

Gambling can become an addiction like drinking alcohol.

It is very easy to start, and many gamblers credit beginners' luck for their addiction. To win a large amount of money the first time one gambles makes the winner believe he/she is lucky.

So emotion soon takes over, and the joyous feeling of winning is hard to forget. It is said that gambling and drugs affect the same area of the brain. It leads the gambler to take risks and lose self-respect. The temptation to gamble is so strong it can turn gamblers into criminals and liars. They will continue even though deep down they know that desire does not change the laws of probability.
Gamblers are usually very kind people who have respectable plans for all the money they hope to win. However, as they start losing, they tend to double their bets to break even, and go broke. The gambler's family members are usually the ones who suffer the most, as addicted betters just cannot stop.

 Many countries and states now run lotteries to raise money for useful projects. They believe that the government can benefit from human weakness as well as the gambling casinos. The media are active supporters of gambling as they publish glowing articles and photos of happy winners. So it's a case of '
a picture is worth a thousand words'. Society would be better served if newspapers showed us some of the people who live in poverty thanks to gambling, or at least reminded us of the odds of 'not being lucky'.

If casinos posted the tremendous odds gamblers have of not winning, it might help to lessen the number of unhappy losers. But it is always very easy to sell hope.

36. Gambling:

Gamblers would probably bet that they can give up gambling and lose. (No pun intended.)

Our earliest ancestors probably gambled using stones or rocks in games of chance or skill. Getting something for nothing, or for very little effort, seems to be part of everyone's DNA. Even the most educated are willing to risk money despite knowing the overwhelming odds against winning. Trying to replicate the powerful feeling of beating the odds is a feeble effort to gain happiness.

Gambling is an addiction similar to alcohol or drugs. The first step is the easiest, and many inveterate gamblers will admit that beginners' luck was their ultimate downfall. Winning is such an emotional high that people want to relive it while believing they were born lucky. Research has shown that drug addiction and gambling stimulate the same area of the brain. The craving for this special thrill often turns gamblers into criminals and clever liars.

So they continue gambling as feelings of hope and memories of past successes are usually strong enough to obliterate common sense or logic.

Generally speaking, gamblers are fine people with the best of intentions. They have very laudable plans for their future winnings. However, losing undermines their ability to think rationally, so they try to recoup their losses by doubling the amount of their wagers. This becomes the express lane to financial ruin. The real victims are usually the gambler's family, as money needed for necessities is sacrificed to the god of chance.

Many governments and states now compete with gambling establishments in order to funnel losers' money into worthwhile projects. Their rationale seems to be :'why should the casino be the sole beneficiary of human weakness and greed?' State run gambling is legitimized further by the media. Newspapers and TV provide great coverage and photos of the happy winners. Truly 'a picture is worth a thousand words.' Society would be better served if we could glimpse the poverty and degradation caused by gambling, or if we were reminded of the astronomical odds against winning.
Similar to cigarette packages, casinos should post the odds gamblers face when betting. It might decrease the suffering and disillusionment that follow this addiction. But selling hope is always in season.

37. Divorce:

Marriage used to mean two people promising to love each other until death. Now that 'death' means until the marriage ends. Indeed, the life of some marriages is often much shorter than the life of the partners promising undying love. Divorce rates seem to be rising in most countries and no one seems to be very worried about it. We trade in cars and motorbikes, so why not trade in spouses too?

It may be worthwhile to look at some of the causes of divorce. First, we should mention the lack of preparation for marriage. Bride and groom are often more interested in the wedding ceremony than in getting ready for the years that follow. In most countries it is harder to get a driver's license than to get a marriage license. Before marriage young people need to realize that successful marriages demand a lot of work, sacrifice, and patience.

Couples who forget that love includes sacrifice and responsible commitment do not remain couples for very long.

Immaturity on the part of one spouse can doom the relationship. Marriage is like a pair of shoes, if only one shoe is comfortable walking is not so pleasant. Two people giving 50% each is another sure recipe for failure. Marriage needs two people giving 100% each, and not comparing whether one's 100% percent is more or less than that of one's partner.

Another reason for divorce is not accepting change. People change as they grow older and hopefully more mature. 'He or she is not the person I married' is just a truism or fact of nature. To maintain a loving and lasting marriage, the mindset must be: 'I love the person you are becoming'.

This guarantees that the couple can happily grow old together and avoid the temptation of pretending to be forever young and attractive.

Another cause of divorce is the TV set. We see actors and actresses seeking happiness in all kinds of extra marital affairs. A constant diet of this can camouflage these evils and make infidelity more palatable to viewers. It is sad to see people viewing TV as an escape from their daily schedule being bombarded with failure dressed up as success and happiness. Communication used to take place around the dinner table, now it is being replaced by TV programs of questionable value.

The final marriage killer is just plain old selfishness. Happiness is never an individual good; it is the byproduct of putting the other first. We see ample examples in failed marriages due to the "me first" syndrome. This unrecognized selfishness usually can ruin even multiple marriages as

Hollywood shamelessly teaches us. The reason given for divorce is usually "incompatibility" which is correct. Compatible means having the ability to suffer, (i.e. to suppress one's ego) to express love. Sadly, some never realize that love has to have this altruistic component.

Grandma was correct when she defined happiness as 'what you receive when you make someone else happy'.

38. Divorce:

Marriage is supposed to be a lifelong commitment between a husband and wife, but now many couples promise to love each other until they sue for divorce. Some marriages do not last much longer than the honeymoon. In many countries the rising divorce rate is accepted like the changing weather. Our disposable materialistic culture now includes throw–away people and institutions as well as throw-away things.

There are a few easily discernible causes for the increasing number of divorces. The most obvious one is lack of preparation on the part of those getting married. Often couples are more interested in the wedding reception than in preparing for their new life together. In most countries it is more difficult to obtain a driver's license that a marriage license. Successful long–lasting marriages do not depend on luck. They are built on the strong foundation of mutual trust, sacrifice, patience, and hard work.

They include a mature level of responsibility which enables the couple to overcome challenges because each spouse puts the happiness of the other first. Marriage is like a pair of shoes; if one shoe is uncomfortable walking is rather unpleasant. Another fallacy is that a successful marriage is two people giving 50% each –like a business arrangement. Marriage should mean two people giving 100% each.

When couples are truly in love they do not measure how much they give.

Another marriage-ending mindset is not accepting change. Expecting one's spouse to be unchanged from the way he/she was before marriage is a stubborn way to reject reality. Mature spouses love the person the other is becoming, with wrinkles, gray hair, or even no hair.

In this way, both partners are not ambushed by fading beauty or the appearance of little faults. Such spouses will not look over their shoulders searching for greener pastures.

The TV can also be blamed for championing divorce. Celebrities in dramas and in real life demonstrate that breaking marriage vows and having as many affairs as possible is the new path to happiness. This subliminal brainwashing gives viewers permission to do likewise, or at least daydream about the possibility.

It is ironic that couples spend precious time facing the TV watching failure, rather than facing each other and laying the foundations for success.

Communication used to mean two people becoming one. Now it can mean two people talking only during commercials.

The final destroyer of marital bliss is selfishness. Happiness is the byproduct of working for the happiness of another. It can never be a solitary selfish experience. A quick recall of recent divorces will prove selfishness is really 'the elephant in the room'. Many Hollywood denizens prove that fame and fortune just exacerbate selfishness rather than conquer it.

As they cite incompatibility as the reason for divorce they are ironically correct. Etymologically, 'compatible' means to suffer and empathize with another to demonstrate love. Unfortunately, some never learn that love is primarily giving not receiving.

My grandma was spot on when she defined happiness as "the scent that stays on your fingers when you pick flowers for someone else."

39. Stress:

Stress can be defined as feeling pressure both in one's mind and body. Sad to say a lot of stress is worry about things that never happen. Stress is living without hope and imagining the worst possible result. So now the question is how can people avoid it, or at least have less of it.

The first step is to find out where stress is coming from. Sometimes it comes from other people, bosses, a spouse, fellow workers, or even the daily news

 For some, it comes from the individual's own personality. Once we know where it comes from, we can take steps to get rid of it.
No being able to forgive is one major stressor. When one is wronged or put down, hate seems like a natural reaction. However, hating someone does nothing good for the one hating. Hate is truly a boomerang. It injures the unforgiving heart more than the person or object hated. Forgiving is what ends stress and restores happiness.

The next step is taking control of one's thoughts, emotions, and imagination. One has to remember that as the boss of one's own life that giving others power to hurt is not healthy.

In the same way, tying one's happiness to a result one cannot control is a useless gamble. Our attitude toward what happens is more important than what happened. Some perfectionists and "yes-men" seem to make stress a welcome visitor in their hearts. Even when everything turns out perfectly, stress lessens their full enjoyment of it.

Stress management offers stressed people ways in which to overcome this problem. Deep breathing, physical exercise, listening to relaxing music, prayer, and meditation are often mentioned as being helpful. For some a combination of two or three possible solutions may prove to be the best way to get rid of stress. Drugs, alcohol, cigarettes, or over eating are thought to be useful in fighting stress when in fact they only increase it.

Believing that stress is a challenge to be met rather than a long lasting problem is the first step to less stress.

40. Stress:

Stress is defined as mental and/or physical tension or pressure caused by a real or imagined problem. It could be classified as the interest we pay for imagining unpleasant scenarios or results. Stress is despair over a potential undesired conclusion. So how can people live stress free or with a minimal amount of it?

First, people have to discover the source of stress. Stressors can be bosses, a spouse, the workplace, or even the daily dose of news. Often it is the 'enemy within' and comes from the personality of the one stressed. Knowledge is power and knowing why one is stressed can be the first step toward curing it.

Stubborn unforgiveness is a major cause of stress. It is easy to justify one's anger at a real or imagined insult or offense. The stress in hating someone (who may deserve it), causes the hater to lose peace and contentment. Hate is a boomerang. It damages the hater much more than the person or object hated. Forgiveness is salutary and a real stress buster.

Next, to be stress free demands conscious control of one's negative thinking, emotional reactions, and pessimistic imagination.

People have to realize that abdicating power over their lives to others is an invitation to make stress a permanent resident in their hearts. Similarly, deciding that happiness depends on the result of a future event is not conducive to a healthy life. Our reaction to happenings is more important than the occurrence itself. "Yes-men" and perfectionists guarantee a never ending supply of stress for themselves. Even when success is achieved or confrontation avoided, full enjoyment of it is tainted by their negative perceptions.

Stress managers offer a number of possible solutions to facilitate stress reduction. Breathing slowly and deeply, physical exercise, listening to relaxing music, and prayerful mediation have all been shown to be beneficial, either individually or in combination. Pseudo remedies such as drugs, alcohol, cigarettes, and over eating just increase stress and should be religiously avoided.

Thinking of stress as a challenge, not as a permanent condition, is the first step to conquering it.

41. The Problem of Evil:
Why do bad things happen to good people?
If God is good where does evil come from? This problem has been discussed for centuries and no one answer has satisfied everyone. If there is no God, where does evil come from? Is there a good God and a bad God? This topic has been around for quite a long time, so we have to start with what we know.

It is easy to see that people can choose. We all have free will (except for the 20 million in the world that are still in slavery.) We choose to do or not do what we want to. We tend to choose everything as "a good". This means that even if people do something mean, hurtful, or something that is against the law, it is chosen as a "good".

For example, I know it is wrong to steal or lie, but at times I may tell myself that stealing is going to make me happy. It is good for me even though I don't want other people to steal from me. Lying is going to help me to look better than I really am, or a lie will help me to escape punishment. At the same time I do not want others to lie to me. To say we are programmed to do evil cannot be proved easily.

We see children raised in the same family who turn out to be either saints or criminals. So genes or environment is not the cause of their choices. As human beings we have a tendency to selfishness, laziness, and greed. If we do not fight against them we will end up as evil people. Fortunately, most people have a little voice in their heart that hints at a perfection we can imagine. This pushes us to accept standards that most of society feels necessary for us to live in peace. So where does evil come from? Possibly from our own selfish choices that if left unchecked can become bad habits. But we may also have to suffer from the bad choices of others as the innocent victims of war can tell us. So blaming God or no God for our misuse of free will is a non-starter.

42. The Problem of Evil:

One of the philosophers' perennial questions is why do good people have to suffer evil?

This dilemma has been around for centuries and still has not been solved to everyone's satisfaction. If there is an omnipotent benevolent loving God, where does evil originate? Some postulate that maybe there are two gods, one malevolent and one benevolent.

We should begin our discussion by mentioning what we know about human nature. People have the ability to make decisions or choose what appeals to them.

This is commonly called 'free will' which is enjoyed by all (except unfortunately by the 20 million people who are kept as slaves.) In selecting our words or actions, we choose them as a good or as a benefit to us.
 (People who can choose evil because it is evil are mentally unbalanced.) So when we acquiesce to evil, which may be selfish, or illegal, it is always under the guise of a good.
For example, I know instinctively that stealing and lying are wrong, but I make an exception for myself when I choose thievery or prevarication to increase my quotient of happiness or to help me avoid deserved punishment or condemnation. The immediate benefit obtained from stealing or lying brings a certain amount of short-lived gratification. However, my self-indulgent attitude is not extended to others who would offend me by appropriating some of my property, or speaking falsely to me. To claim that people are helpless to resist evil is not borne out by tangible experience or evidence.
We sometimes see siblings, even twins, who have so much in common, end up as either paragons of virtue or despicable criminals.

So environment or genes cannot explain the discrepancies between these family members. As human beings we have a tendency to selfishness, laziness, and greed. Unless we resist the attractiveness of these vices we may end up as truly evil people.

Fortunately, we also possess the voice of conscience which allows us to imagine a perfect society, or at least acceptable standards for dealing with each other. We postulate a moral law that is the lubrication of social interactions. So where does evil come from? It is caused by the exercise of free will that compromises with evil and enshrines it as a good. It can be our own free will or that of others which directly causes most of our sufferings in this world. The innocent victims of war sadly but eloquently bear testimony to this truth.

So blaming God or no God for the problem of evil is not the answer

43. Thanks, No Thanks:

When I go shopping, I often have to wait in line at the checkout counter. To kill time I count the number of people who say 'thank you' to the cashier. My unofficial survey results have surprised me. About one in ten say 'thank you', and some of those should not be counted as they may be friends of the store employee.

So now we have to find out the causes of this new reality in our society. There are three possible reasons for this lack of manners.

First, many put a monetary value on everything, so 'thank you' is not worth anything. So it is natural to conclude that even saying it is a waste of time. Secondly, in the same vein, everything that is bought is paid for, so why should people thank someone for taking their money?

The customer is directly or indirectly paying the store employee's salary, so he or she deserves a 'thank you' for going to that store.

Thirdly, people spending money usually feel superior to those who provide a service, and thanking them is turning the social order upside down. TV strongly reinforces our lack of politeness. When we see politicians or leaders in action, they conveniently forget to express thanks.

People open doors for them, provide them with food and drink, and even help them to sit down. Showing respect for their position in society is expected, but hearing a word of thanks from them is not expected. When this is repeated over time we will have an unnoticed change in our culture. So in a short span of time 'thank you' will be a forgotten word.

44. Thanks, No Thanks:

Waiting in line at the supermarket provides me with an excellent opportunity to observe my fellow shoppers. Recently I have begun compiling statistics on how many customers express their appreciation or gratitude to the cashier. The results of this non-scientific survey have amazed me. Less than 10% of customers express their gratitude to the sales staff.

So now I want to ascertain why this is happening or to be more precise – not happening. There are at least three obvious reasons for this lack of gratitude. The first is that nowadays everything is assigned a monetary value, and 'thank you' is considered to have none. So thanking an employee becomes meaningless. It is a waste of time and time is money!

Secondly, consumers are spending their hard earned money in a store, and thanking sales people for accepting their money is unnecessary. On the contrary, the shoppers expect to be thanked for choosing that store! After all, they may feel that their purchasing is contributing to the sales staff's salaries.

Thirdly, those spending money tend to feel much higher in the social order than those providing a service. (The old master slave mentality is subconsciously alive and well.)

TV brainwashes us into not even noticing a lack of politeness. Business leaders, CEOs, politicians, and even celebrities are catered to by all of us.

We open doors for them, help them find the best seats, and provide other acts of politeness but appreciation is never expressed or even expected. Constantly seeing such 'thankless' scenes will subconsciously change our culture. In one more generation 'thank you' may be as dead as the dodo bird.

45. Self-Esteem:

Present day American high school students have a very high opinion of themselves. They think they are smart and above average in many areas, and they feel that they should be appreciated more. However, in a recent test with students from 30 other countries, the Americans came in last or almost last in all the subjects tested.

One could say their high regard for their abilities is not based on results.

This 'feel good about oneself' movement began about 30 years ago, and it was never based on what one did to deserve to feel good. Students were spoiled, praised, and put on a pedestal just because they were born.

This band wagon of self-esteem began in schools, and insecure parents quickly jumped on board to increase its momentum. Once they got rid of hard work and real competition, selfishness soon filled the vacuum caused by 'easier said but never done.'

Of course all this was done to help the child. The child's feelings were thought to be most important, and parents knelt before the altar of praise they had built for their offspring. Recognizing faults, pointing out areas of weakness, and even saying 'no' to a child were all consigned to the garbage dump of bad parenting. Compliments became the new way to communicate, and expecting little protected the weak egos of spoiled children. The little princes and princesses wallowed in so much empty praise that their self-loving little hearts grow bigger. The campaign went full circle and returned back to the schools that began it.

Cowardly teachers gave out grades like presents from a store Santa, and non-competitive feel-good education was in vogue.

Students got a good grade for just being present, and taking part in a sport meant everyone got a trophy. Standards were thought to be dangerous for students, especially for those who were doing poorly. Teachers rushed to psychology books to find support for their new ideas of stress-free education. This noisy pseudoscience group drowned out common sense as feelings replaced performance.

While this new thinking reminds us of the story of the naked emperor's clothes, it should be noted that low self-esteem is not very useful. Students can be shackled by false beliefs about themselves, over sensitive about their appearance, suffer from negative peer pressure, mean parents, and being expected to achieve unrealistic goals.

However, the answer to low self- esteem is not self-respect gained from exaggerated praise and imagined success. Hollywood loves to hand out fame and fortune to those who can act well, while their personal lives often leave a lot to be desired. This hardly seems like a constructive example to offer students on the road to success.

Parents and teachers must realize that high self-esteem does not guarantee great success. Confidence has to be based on many small successful steps taken with perseverance and hard work. When students realize that ability is strengthened by tough competition they will experience earned self-esteem. Trying to "be all you can be" is not only the army's motto, but good advice for students starting out.

Allowing students to experience difficult work that demands effort with no guarantee of success is the key to their becoming mature citizens. It is healthy to believe one can succeed; it foolish to believe one can succeed without trying.

46. Self Esteem:

A recent survey announced that American students' self-esteem is at an all-time high. They feel that they are more talented, more capable, more intellectual, and of course most lovable than at any time in history. So this feeling good about themselves seems to contradict the fact that when tested with students from 30 other countries, American students came last or close to last in most subjects tested. So much for self-esteem based on performance.

This obsession with self–admiration divorced from performance can be traced back to the self-esteem movement that began about three decades ago. Students were coddled, lauded, and applauded for their uniqueness- which is a euphemism for being born.

It began in schools and it was adopted by insecure parents whose idea of love excluded all discipline. Once effort and competition were sufficiently denigrated, narcissism rushed in to fill the vacuum.

Of course all this was created with the best of intentions. The feelings of the child were so precious that father and mother became cheerleaders instead of parents.

Criticism, blame, correction, and even the word" no" became anathema. Encomiastic comments rained down on mediocre effort as fragile egos were cocooned in layers of low expectations. The little princes and princesses raised in such a rarefied atmosphere believed the empty words and loved themselves even more. It even boomeranged back to the schools.
Teachers were afraid to have standards and good grades were handed out like stickers in child care centers. The non-competitive philosophy of education emerged. Everyone got rewarded for participation; everyone got a trophy for playing

Objective standards were mocked and viewed as pernicious attacks on underperforming students. Educators —or rather those who should be educators - rushed to psychology to legitimize arguments that their non-education was really a success. Their incessant ranting and pseudoscience carried the day as feelings trumped performance.

While exaggerated self-esteem has proved to be the naked emperor's latest fashion in attire, it reminds us that low self-esteem does damage students and children. A youngster's perception of self can be influenced by his/her appearance, peer pressure, abusive parents, and unreal expectations.

However, the antidote to low self-esteem is not self-esteem based on nothing but evanescent words that promote delusions of success.   -212-

The Hollywood celebrity culture bestows prizes and fame on those who can act successfully in dramas or movies, while their personal lives are often in shambles. So is this the example we offer students on the road to success?

First, parents and teachers must realize that an excess of self-esteem does not translate into an excess of success.

Confidence comes from a series of small achievements gained through diligence and hard work. When students realize that they each have ability that can be improved through competition, they will develop earned self-esteem. The old army motto: "Be all you can be" dictates the first step towards a healthy self-respect. The process should be letting students experience effort, responsibility, and even failure as we help them to mature. Belief in one's potential is healthy; belief that one has a monopoly on genius is disastrous.

47. Fish to Die for:

In Japan good fish can cost a lot of money but one fish can cost diners their life. Connoisseurs of fine food consider the fugu or puffer fish as a most special delicacy. It is served raw (sashimi) and it is supposed to be very tasty. If the chef makes a mistake it its preparation, it can be a diner's final taste.

The innards of this fish are poisonous and can cause permanent heart failure. If eaten sparingly it delivers a numbing feeling to the lips which is the thrill that fugu eaters risk their lives for. However, knowing how much to eat can be a matter of life or death. Last year while enjoying this delicacy, 17 brave diners got very sick while one was not so lucky.

The Japanese government is trying to make fugu-eating safe, but it can only do so much. They require fugu chefs to be licensed. Five years of training and a tough graduation test are required. All those rules do not stop amateurs from preparing their own fish -often with deadly results.

As many people wish to consume this dangerous fish, the government is now allowing most restaurants to serve frozen fugu. This will let them compete with the Internet and black market sales. It should lessen the number of deaths from fugu poisoning but some hard to please gourmets will still risk eating the poisonous parts.
If I want to have a numb lip I will visit my dentist.

48. Fish to Die for:

Good fish can be expensive, but Japan literally has a fish to die for. Gourmets rate the fugu or puffer fish a special treat. It is usually served as sashimi or raw fish, the taste of which is supposed to be out of this world. But if prepared incorrectly, it will take diners out of this world.
The internal organs of the puffer fish contain toxins which can prove fatal. If taken in small amounts, it causes a tingling or numbing sensation in the lips. This anesthetic effect thrills the palate of puffer fish aficionados.

However, knowing how much of the poisonous parts to eat is like playing Russian roulette. Last year, 17 courageous diners barely cheated death, while one succumbed from eating this expensive treat.

The Japanese government tries to prevent fatalities but regulations do not guarantee success. They have made it mandatory that chefs who serve fugu be licensed. Rigorous training takes about five years, and the graduation test is quite difficult.   -214-

Of course this does not stop amateurs from slicing up their own fish, often with disastrous consequences. To meet the growing demand for puffer fish, the government is relaxing some of its stringent regulations. Frozen fugu will be available even in restaurants without a licensed chef. This will allow them to compete with Internet and black market sales.

Besides, this will prevent poisoning the consumers. Still some extreme gourmets will demand the thrilling numbing taste of the toxic parts. Personally, if I want to feel my lip tingling, my dentist is always available.

49. Smoking:

Smoking in public should be against the law. Smoking is a personal action that affects other people whether they like it or not. Often, an innocent person walking down the street is attacked by dirty smoke coming from a smoker's lungs. This limits the freedom of the one walking even though the attack is not done on purpose. Even in a free country, there are certain things one cannot do. For example, one cannot walk down the street swinging a hammer. Other people have a right to be safe, and that precedes any hammer–swinging right. How come it is not the same for smoking? Consequently, we need better laws.

Smoking is not a harmless activity like whistling or singing in public. The singer may anger listeners– especially if he or she has a bad voice- but the smoker directly impacts health. Second hand smoke has been known to cause cancer. One argument for smoker's rights mentions that not everyone gets cancer.

However, this does not make much sense. For example, if a factory spews out dangerous gases, it is liable for the damage done to the health of people in that area, no matter whether they all get sick or not. People have a right to be safe and to safeguard their health. Smoking ignores that right as it is inherently dangerous.

Smoking is not just a personal bad habit; it affects everyone directly and indirectly. When a person smokes, he/she runs the risk of increasing the severity of any existing health problems. This eventually leads to more sick days, more hospital visits, higher insurance costs for all, and less work.

As a result, we can put a monetary value on the damage done to society by smokers. This is without even thinking about the pain and damage done to their children, spouses, and friends.
Thus, the damage to society caused by smoking must be stressed repeatedly so our children are well informed. But we cannot depend on the government to help in this campaign; they make a lot of money taxing the sale of cigarettes.

50 Smoking:

Legislatures should ban smoking in public places. This personal right to smoke has ramifications that involve other people irrespective of their feelings about smoking. An innocent pedestrian can become the victim of smoke being expelled from a smoker's unhealthy lungs.

This curtails the victim's freedom even though the attack is not premeditated or even intended. Even in a free country there are limits to freedom. For example, one cannot walk around swinging a hammer or other danger tool. People have a right to safety that supersedes any hammer swinging right. Is it too far-fetched to apply the same principle to smoking in public?

We need better legislation to protect us.

Smoking is not an innocuous pastime similar to whistling or singing in public. The singer may irritate listeners, especially if he or she is not endowed with a good voice, but the smoker directly affects health. Even second hand smoke is a carcinogen. Some who favor smoking may argue that not every victim gets cancer. However, there is a fallacy in this line of reasoning. If a factory spews out poisonous gases it is liable for the damage done to the health of those in that locality, irrespective of whether everyone succumbs to ill health or not. Unlike the time of the industrial revolution, citizens now have a right to clean air. Smoking in public infringes on that right and is intrinsically dangerous.

Inhaling and exhaling smoke is not just an individual's bad habit, it has far- reaching repercussions. First, it exacerbates existing health problems the smoker may have. This results in more hospital visits, the consumption of more medicines, higher medical insurance premiums, and less productive labor. Consequently, we can put a monetary value on the effects of cigarettes. This does not even take into consideration the pain and problems suffered by spouses, children, and friends of the smoker. The tremendous damage caused by smoking must be broadcast far and wide, long and loud until all get the message, especially the next generation. But do not expect the government to be involved; they make money taxing cigarette sales.

51. What Is Learned From Foreign Travel:

When students from Japan travel outside Japan, and indeed anyone who travels to a foreign country, their reactions seems to be predictable. The most often heard comment is :"I learned a lot about foreign culture." It is surprising how much they learn from a few weeks outside their own borders. Perhaps they do learn a little due to some misunderstandings or difficulties, but what they really learned is the opposite.

The first thing they learn is what it means to be Japanese, or what it means to be a citizen of their own country. They are without their usual support system, familiar language, and are faced with different ways of doing things. As a result, they experience a kind of unpleasant feeling of not fitting in. It could be compared to a person who likes to wear clothes, being forced to go naked in a nudist colony.

Or it could be compared to a fish out of water. The fish probably does not realize it is surrounded by water until it is removed from it. So short time visitors to foreign countries should be able to relate to the fish.

When one lives in one's country of birth, the culture, values, language, religion, and humor are all part of a common heritage. There is no comparison with those of foreign countries. People grow up with the mores of their community and that gives them the ability to function easily as citizens of that state or nation. Upon leaving their own surroundings, everything changes in a big way. They are forced to rethink their values and ways of doing things as they see others living what they consider normal lives.

Japanese students can react in one of three ways. First, they can be attracted to the values of foreigners and reject their own culture.

Or, they can resist the foreign ways of thinking and doing, and count the days until they can go home.

Thirdly, they can selectively appreciate some parts of the new culture and maybe even think about adopting them. Either way, they are forced to learn the essentials of their own culture which is a big step toward maturity. So the next time, when someone asks about the lessons you learned from travel, I hope your answer will be: "I learned what it means to be a citizen of my own country"

What is Learned from Foreign Travel:

51. The reactions of Japanese students and even foreign students to overseas travel seem to be scripted. "I learned all about foreign culture" seems to be the exaggerated appraisal of using their passports. It is quite amazing how much culture is assimilated in a short sojourn outside one's own country.

 Of course a modicum of cultural knowledge is often learned from unpleasant misunderstandings and faux pas made by first time travelers. What is really understood is usually overlooked, namely, what it means to be a citizen of one's own country.

When deprived of cultural and ethnic supports (taken for granted at home), one faces new unknown challenges never before imagined.

Having difficulties understanding the language, not knowing the why or how of new etiquette, and trying to meet unknown expectations, all force visitors to clearly grasp the meaning and extent of their own culture. Feeling like a fish out of water or imaging oneself naked before one's peers may provide an idea of what this disorientation feels like.

While living in one's own country, language, culture, religion, and values are like the air. They are no comparisons envisioned, life is comfortable, and security is taken for granted.

In a foreign country, citizens there consider their way of life as normal, even though it may be completely different to what visitors are used to. So visitors are forced to experience differences while lacking understanding of the ethos that undergirds them.

Japanese or other travelers may react to the new culture in any of three ways. They may embrace the new culture while becoming critical of their own culture and values. A second possible reaction is to selectively adopt some values and incorporate them into their own values. The only other possibility is to reject the foreign culture and thank God one has a return ticket.

No matter which path is chosen, the traveler is forced to acknowledge and relearn his/her own culture. So the best answer to the perennial question of what was learned by leaving one own country would be: "I now know what it means to be a citizen of my own country."

The Many Meanings of Make:

1. He makes chairs. She makes dresses. I made breakfast.

2. I tried to get into Harvard; I didn't make it. I wanted to play soccer but I didn't make the team. I can make your party tomorrow. (succeed, attend).

3. He will never make Kyoto in two hours. (get to). I made good time en route. (came quickly). 3B. What will we order? Let's make it tempura. (decide on).

4. Sugihara Chiune made a difference, but he didn't make any money.   (He helped many but never got rich.)

5. That last strike-out makes 10 in all. (totals). One hundred cents makes a dollar. In golf, he made a birdie…she made a split…a goal. (scored).

6. Someone made off with my bike. (stole). How did you make out in the interview? (do). Make the most of your time in school. (Use it well).

7. The government makes laws to make the people happy. Some laws make me cry…laugh. My apartment needs a makeover. (to be fixed up). If you are late for class make something up. (Make up an excuse.)

8. 'He likes beer.' 'That makes two of us!' (I do too.) He made light of my problem. (He thought it was not serious.)

 9. Make yourself at home here. (relax). He makes it a habit of coming late.

10. Make room for one more student. He did extra homework to make up for missing class. (to balance).

11. They had a fight but they made up soon after it.
   (They forgave each other.)

12. I don't know what to make of this email. (I cannot understand it.)

Idioms:

1. Your son is just talking to a girl. Don't <u>jump to conclusions</u>.
 (Don't think it is a serious relationship.)

2. Those loose steps are just <u>an accident waiting to happen</u>.
(The steps are dangerous.)

3. Buying cigarettes for her son <u>goes against the grain</u>.
(It's against her values.)

4. He never works. He should <u>get his act together</u>.
(He should be responsible and work.)

5. That couple always fight. Don't <u>add fuel to the fire</u>.
(Don't say anything to make it worse.)

6. He succeeded <u>beyond my wildest dreams</u>.
(I never expected him to do so well.)

7. Your <u>best bet is</u> to go shopping early in the morning; more parking! (It's best to go early.)

8. Since he retired he has become <u>a couch potato.</u>
(He just sits on the couch and gets fatter.)

9. I <u>bumped into</u> a classmate in Tokyo. It's a small world.
(I met my classmate by accident – unplanned.)

10. The company is giving workers a 3% raise <u>across the board</u>. (Every worker will get a 3% increase in salary.)

11. I'm tired; <u>let's call it a day.</u> (Let's stop and go home.)

12.What's going on here? <u>What's going on</u> with your new job. (What is happening? How is your new job?)

13. You did your best. <u>Don't sweat it.</u> (Don't worry about it.)

14. I was <u>under the weather</u> for a few days. Now I'm fine. (I was not feeling well.)

15. He said he is broke, but I <u>don't buy</u> that. He plays pachinko every day. (I don't believe it. I don't accept that.)

16. We're leaving at 1:00 <u>on the dot.</u> Don't be late! (We are leaving at exactly 1:00 o'clock.)

17. <u>It beats me</u> how he can afford that car. (I don't understand.)

18. A.“It's cold today.” B. “<u>You can say that again.</u> (I agree 100%.)

19. Farmers are the salt of the earth. (Farmers are very good and necessary people.)

20. Let me <u>pick your brains</u> about Tokyo. Weren't you born there? (I want your advice about Tokyo.)

21. My friends are <u>dead set against</u> my renting rooms in my home. (They think it is a bad idea.)

22. Raising kids on one salary <u>is no picnic</u>. (It is not easy.)

23.There is a lot of <u>red tape</u> when you deal with the city hall. (There is a lot of paperwork.)

24. Putting a flower bed in front of that ugly building is like <u>putting lipstick on a pig</u>. (The flowers will not make it pretty.)

25. He stole your pen because it's green. "That's <u>beside the point</u> . (That's a crazy reason; he shouldn't have done it.)

26. She's always late so I'll <u>give her a taste of her own medicine</u>.   (I'll be late this time.)

27. Sometimes the teacher <u>goes off on a tangent</u>. (He/she talks about topics not related to class.)

28. Learning English <u>will pay dividends</u> later. (It will prove worthwhile.)

29. He always <u>picks up the tab</u> when we eat out. (He always pays the bill.)

30. I <u>gave</u> Mr. Sun <u>a piece of my mind</u> about parking in front of my gate. (I scolded him severely for blocking my entrance.)

31. He <u>got the message</u>. Now he parks in a parking lot. (He understood what I said.)

32. She lets her children <u>get away with murder</u> (They do what they like. There is no discipline.)

33. I have to work many jobs to <u>make ends meet.</u> (Just to live I do many jobs.)

34. She will go bowling <u>at the drop of a hat.</u> (She is always eager and ready to go bowling.)

35. He will <u>go the extra mile</u> with you. (He will do more than you expect.)

36. He went to the funeral <u>to save face</u>. (For appearances- to keep others from talking about his absence.)

37. I think I'll <u>hit the road</u>. (I will leave or go home.)

38. The new teacher is <u>on the ball</u>. (Very efficient.)

39. My typing <u>leaves a lot to be desired</u>. (It is not good.)

40. I'm sleepy; time to <u>hit the sack.</u> (Time to go to bed.)

******